Music & Lyrics by
Adam Spiegel

Book & Lyrics by
David Spiegel & Stacy Davidowitz

STEELE SPRING
STAGE RIGHTS

www.stagerights.com

For all stage performance inquiries, please contact:

Steele Spring Stage Rights
3845 Cazador Street
Los Angeles, CA 90065 (323) 739-0413
www.stagerights.com

CHARACTERS

SAN JUAN HILL CAMPERS

BRIAN "PLAY DOUGH" GARFINK: An unapologetic, extroverted leader of the cabin; loud, magnetic personality; dopey with a hint of comedic timing; loves to eat; 12.

ROBERT STEINBERG: A robot-loving, adopted Jewish-Asian bookworm with asthma; 12.

JUSTIN "TOTLE" PETERSON: An obtuse, philosophical jock with incredible hand-eye coordination; 12.

ERNEST "WIENER" MEYER: A truth-stretcher with sympathetic eagerness, loyalty, and a heart of gold; "bumped up" an age-level to be with his friends; 11.

BENJAMIN DOVER: An Eagle Scout with skilled, dire commitment to prank efficiency; 12.

ROBERT "SMELLY" BENJAMIN: A new camper with a love for baseball, and an acquired love for guitar; the underdog; 12.

ANITA HILL CAMPERS

STACY MELMAN: Once a tomboy, has blossomed into a down-to-earth athletic beauty; pragmatic, a realist; 12.

MELISSA "MISSI" SNYDER: A cat-loving, marching band sort of girl who would love to be "in" with Jamie and Jenny; 12.

STEPHANIE "SLIMEY" GREGSON: A sweet, mature, compassionate "every girl" with an introverted, artistic side; 12.

JENNIFER "JENNY" NOLAN: A ditsy, gossipy dancer-type with the cutest-ever boyfriend at home; best friends forever and ever with Jamie; 12.

JAMIE NEDERBAUER: A ditsy, gossipy wannabe dancer-type without a cutest-ever boyfriend; best friends forever and ever with Jenny; 12.

SOPHIE EDGERSTECKIN: A supernatural-romance-loving, journal-writing know-it-all with severe allergies to almost everything; 12.

CHARACTERS (CONT'D)

ROLLING HILLS STAFF

RICK ROLAND: San Juan Hill boys' counselor, once camper; friendly, laissez-faire attitude, respectful; plays the guitar; 17.

SARA PETERSON: Anita Hill girls' counselor, once a camper; angsty, emotional; wittily pessimistic with the potential for happiness; 18.

KERRI "CAPTAIN" JEREKI: Camp Director; a conservative leaning, old-fashioned disciplinarian at times, a goof at others; previous experience in the navy; married to Ted; 40-60.

TED "TJ" JEREKI: Camp Director by marital association; loves the sound of his own voice, a kid at heart; married to Kerri; 40-60.

Casting is flexible when it comes to age. Young actors or adult actors could play any of the roles. Plausibly, adults could play the campers and young performers could play the camp directors. Have fun!

TECHNICAL REQUIREMENTS

The set can be as minimal or as elaborate as the director sees fit. The musical works well with three beds or bunk beds mounted on individual rotating boards that, when rotated, represent the beds of either the boys or girls cabin. The beds can be realistically sized or smaller, depending on how they are utilized by the actors. Rotating flats representing the boys and girls cabins can be used to supplement the beds. When there is a split scene and both cabins are on stage at once, two of the beds/flats can be rotated to represent the boys' side and one can be rotated to represent the girls' side or vice-versa. Other set pieces include a curtain to represent the entrance of the counselors' nooks, a baseball base (first base), a newcomb net, a suggestion of a supply closet, and a suggestion of a stage for the talent show.

SET DECORATIONS

Cubbies of clothes
Sports equipment
Posters (a cat one, especially)
General cabin "stuff"
Food wrappers
Fishing supplies

RUNNING TIME

1 hour and 45 minutes

ROLLING HILLS

MUSICAL NUMBERS

ACT I

1. ROLLING HILLS..Campers, Staff
2. NICKNAME.. San Juan Hill Campers (Boys)
3. BOYFRIEND...Anita Hill Campers (Girls)
4. EVERYBODY'S GOOD AT SOMETHING ....Rick & Smelly
5. LETTER WRITING .... Campers (Boys & Girls)
5a. STEINBERG'S LETTER ....Steinberg
6. A REASON TO SMILE ....Slimey & Smelly
7. BACKSTAGE .... Jenny, Play Dough, Jamie
8. SLOW SONG .... TJ, Captain, Campers

ACT II

9. ALMA MATER ....Dover, Play Dough, Steinberg, Totle, Wiener
10. RAID .... San Juan Hill Campers (Boys)
10a. GIRLS' RAID ....Anita Hill Campers (Girls)
10b. RAID FINALE .... Campers (Boys & Girls)
11. ALL THE SONGS ON MY IPOD MAKE ME THINK OF YOU .... Smelly, Slimey
12. CHICKS BEFORE BOYS .... Jenny, Jamie
13. A DIFFERENT DEFINITION OF COOL............... San Juan Hill Campers (Boys)
14. IPOD REPRISE ....Smelly
15. IT'S ALWAYS SUMMER SOMEWHERE ....Rick, Sara, Campers
16. ROLLING HILLS REPRISE / FINALE ....Campers, Staff

ACT I

SCENE 1

CAMP ROLLING HILLS

A serene, wooded campground in Upstate New York. It is the first day of summer camp. Music up.

> *Robert STEINBERG, a lanky, Asian adolescent wearing glasses and a BIG backpack, enters, rolling in a large trunk. He stops, drops the trunk, runs across the stage, breathes in the fresh air.*

STEINBERG: Camp air smells different, it really, really—

> *STEINBERG sneezes three times, takes a puff out of his inhaler, then sits on the trunk to recuperate.*

(Singing)
READY FOR THE SUMMER
HERE AT ROLLING HILLS
I'VE BEEN THINKIN 'BOUT IT EVERY DAY
AT FIRST I THOUGHT THERE WOULD BE ROBOTS
BUT THERE WEREN'T ANY ROBOTS
BUT SOMEHOW I LIKED IT ANYWAY.

> *SOPHIE Edgersteckin, an anxious, journal-writing adolescent, enters reading a vampire love story, "Howling at the Sun" by Georgina Whitefoot. She stops short when she sees STEINBERG.*

SOPHIE: Oh, hey Steinberg! I didn't know you were here already. The buses haven't come in yet, have they?

STEINBERG: My parents dropped me off. Even when the Dramamine settles my nausea, the bus fumes tighten my lungs.

SOPHIE: You're special just like me!

(Singing)
JUST FLEW IN FROM FLORIDA
WITHOUT MY PARENTS
BUT THEY MADE ME TAKE MY EPIPEN
'CAUSE SOMETIMES AIRPLANES GIVE YOU PEANUTS
BUT I CAN'T EAT ANY PEANUTS
OR I'LL PROB'LY NEVER BREATHE AGAIN.

SOPHIE (CONT'D):
WOW MY HEART'S BEATING
THINK I'M OVERHEATING
STEINBERG:
TIME TO START GREETING
SOPHIE & STEINBERG:
HEY THE BUS IS ROLLING IN
NOW THE SUMMER CAN BEGIN

The remaining campers have arrived!

CAMPERS:
LOVE TO SEE THOSE ROLLING HILLS
THE SUN IS SHINING, I GOT CHILLS
WAITED TEN LONG MONTHS
BUT SCHOOL IS OUT AT LAST
AND ALL MY FRIENDS ARE HERE
FOR ANOTHER SUMMER AT CAMP
YEAH, ANOTHER SUMMER AT CAMP
TOTLE:
TIRED OF MY HOMEWORK
PLAY DOUGH:
AND ORGANIC HEALTH FOOD
DOVER:
AND MY STUPID SISTER BETHANY
STEINBERG:
SICK OF OVERBEARING PARENTS
WELL, I MEAN, I LOVE MY PARENTS
BUT SOMETIMES THEY JUST BOTHER ME
WIENER:
NO MORE COMPLAININ'
STEINBERG:
OR BAR MITZVAH TRAININ'
PLAY DOUGH:
NO MORE WEIGHT MAINTAININ'
BOYS:
COULDN'T WAIT UNTIL TODAY
NOW IT'S FINALLY TIME TO SAY
I CAN SEE THOSE ROLLING HILLS
THE SUN IS SHINING, I GOT CHILLS
WAITED TEN LONG MONTHS
BUT SCHOOL IS OUT AT LAST
AND ALL MY FRIENDS ARE HERE

BOYS (CONT'D):
>FOR ANOTHER SUMMER AT CAMP
>YEAH, ANOTHER SUMMER AT CAMP

JAMIE:
>HOPE I GET A BOYFRIEND

SOPHIE:
>HOPE I DON'T GET HOMESICK

MELMAN:
>GONNA TRY MY HAND AT TETHERBALL

SLIMEY:
>GONNA ORGANIZE THE CABIN

JENNY:
>MAKE A LOT OF THINGS WITH LANYARD

MISSI:
>AND PLASTER POSTERS ON MY WALL

SOPHIE:
>I AM DE-LIGHTED

MISSI:
>FINALLY REUNITED

JAMIE & JENNY:
>WE'RE LIKE SO EXCITED

MELMAN:
>COULDN'T WAIT UNTIL TODAY

SLIMEY:
>NOW IT'S FINALLY TIME TO SAY...

GIRLS:
>LOVE TO SEE THOSE ROLLING HILLS
>THE SUN IS SHINING, I GOT CHILLS
>WAITED TEN LONG MONTHS
>BUT SCHOOL IS OUT AT LAST
>AND ALL MY FRIENDS ARE HERE
>FOR ANOTHER SUMMER AT CAMP
>YEAH, ANOTHER SUMMER AT CAMP

INSTRUMENTAL

TJ and CAPTAIN speak over the PA.

TJ: Good morning Camp Rolling Hills! Can I get a rrrrooollling hills?

CAMPERS: Rolling Hills!

TJ: And welcome or welcome back, whichever it is, you're welcome! We're pumped like limitless ketchup you are here with us ahora. This is going to be an AMAAAA...

CAPTAIN: TJ? You're gonna break the mic—

TJ: ...ZING summer!

> *RICK, 17, the boys' counselor, and SARA, 18, the girls' counselor, enter.*

RICK: San Juan Hill Cabin over here please!

SARA: If you're in Anita Hill Cabin you're with me! Get a move on!

> *TJ and CAPTAIN continue on the PA.*

TJ: Find your groups and get ready to have the time of your lives!

CAPTAIN: Dinner's at six today—

TJ *(butchering an Italian accent)*: A'spaghetti and a'meatballs.

CAPTAIN: I'd have abs of steel if it weren't so irresistibly delicious.

TJ: Oh, Captain, you do have abs of—

> *PA goes off with a sharp squeal.*

CAMPERS & STAFF:
> LOVE TO SEE THOSE ROLLING HILLS
> THE SUN IS SHINING, I GOT CHILLS
> WAITED TEN LONG MONTHS
> BUT SCHOOL IS OUT AT LAST
> AND ALL MY FRIENDS ARE HERE
> FOR ANOTHER SUMMER AT CAMP
> YEAH, ANOTHER SUMMER AT CAMP

> *Robert Benjamin, soon to be known as SMELLY, enters. He's wearing a little league baseball t-shirt and cap, and lugging a heavy, wheel-less trunk and struggling. He asks another boy, a chubby one that everyone calls PLAY DOUGH, for help.*

SMELLY: Excuse me? Can you help me? I'm looking for San Juan Hill Cabin?

PLAY DOUGH: No way! That's our cabin!

WIENER: We've got a new kid!

BOYS:
> WE WELCOME YOU TO ROLLING HILLS
> WE ROLL, YOU ROLL WITH US
> IF LOYAL TO YOUR CABINMATES
> WE'RE GLAD TO ADD A PLUS
> CAMP ROLLING HILLS
> OUR HOME FORE'ER YOU'LL BE
> IN THE BOSOM OF THE VALLEY
> SUN SHINES OVER THEE
> CAMP ROLLING HILLS
> FIRM OUR LOYALTY
> MAY OUR HEARTS BE FILLED FOREVER WITH THY MEMORY

SMELLY:
>LIFE WAS FINE TILL MY PARENTS WENT AND SPLIT
>THEY GOT A DIVORCE,
>NOW I'M STUCK IN THIS PIT
>THESE KIDS ARE WEIRD, I'M ALL ALONE
>THEY DON'T HAVE INTERNET
>AND I CAN'T USE MY PHONE

WIENER:
>MAN, THOSE GIRLS LOOK FINE
>HOPE I MAKE ONE MINE

PLAY DOUGH: Dude, when's lunch?

SLIMEY:
>IT'S MY FAVORITE TIME OF YEAR

SMELLY:
>SOMEONE GET ME OUTTA HERE!

CAMPERS & STAFF:
>LOVE TO SEE THOSE ROLLING HILLS
>THE SUN IS SHINING, I GOT CHILLS
>WAITED TEN LONG MONTHS
>BUT SCHOOL IS OUT AT LAST
>AND ALL MY FRIENDS ARE HERE
>FOR ANOTHER SUMMER AT CAMP
>YEAH, ANOTHER SUMMER AT CAMP
>YEAH, ANOTHER SUMMER AT CAMP
>YEAH, ANOTHER SUMMER AT CAMP

SCENE 2

BOYS' CABIN (SAN JUAN HILL CABIN)

A clean cabin with three sets of unmade bunk beds and accompanying sets of cubbies. There is a curtain where a door might be, suggesting a counselor nook, and a guitar propped up nearby. This is RICK's.

This is the cleanest we will see the cabin; as the show progresses, the mess will grow and the BOYS will work around it.

Enter RICK followed by the BOYS minus SMELLY.

PLAY DOUGH: Shot top bunk!

WIENER: No way! You can't have top bunk, you'll crush me.

PLAY DOUGH: No, I won't.

STEINBERG: Deriving a conclusion based on simple physics, you will.

DOVER: Driving a contusion based on past experience, you will.

TOTLE: Oh, man. Remember when we were all chilling on Dover's top bunk and Play Dough climbed up and the whole bunk bed collapsed?

PLAY DOUGH: Fine— then Wiener, as the baby of the cabin you can bunk with the new kid.

WIENER: I'll be 12 soon.

PLAY DOUGH: Yeah, like next year. Steinberg will sleep below me.

STEINBERG: Can't. Asthma. The dust.

RICK: Hey guys, what happened to Robert?

STEINBERG: I'm right here.

RICK: No, the other Robert.

> *The door opens. SMELLY, panting, hurls a heavy trunk into the room.*

SMELLY: This place has a lotta hills.

PLAY DOUGH: You know, they bring your trunks for you.

RICK: Don't worry about it, buddy. Guys, help Robert with his stuff, okay? Show him how neatly you all unpack.

WIENER *(carrying a stack of folded shirts)*: I color coordinate my shirts on occasion. Just so I really know what my options are when I get dressed in the morning.

> *PLAY DOUGH dumps WIENER's clothes to the floor.*

WIENER: Come on!

SMELLY: Is that your guitar?

RICK: Yes, sir.

SMELLY: Cool. Can I try it?

RICK: Later. First, cubby your folded clothes. Start strong, boys. I'll be out on the porch if anyone needs me.

> *RICK exits.*

WIENER: Hey newbie, I gotta be on bottom for easy access. So climb on top like a cop.

TOTLE: I didn't know cops share bunk beds.

SMELLY: Easy access to what?

PLAY DOUGH: To the bathroom. He's a bed-wetter.

WIENER: No! It's 'cause I gotta have easy access to the door, so I can sneak out.

PLAY DOUGH: Dude-a-cris, you don't have a girlfriend.

STEINBERG: Dude-a-cris? Cool.

WIENER: Yeah, but did you see Melman? Holy turds, she got hot.

STEINBERG: Holy turds?

WIENER: Yeah, I'm trying it.

PLAY DOUGH: Don't.

SMELLY: Which one is Melman?

DOVER: Baseball hat, cargo shorts.

WIENER: And the most penetrating eyes.

TOTLE: Penetrating how?

PLAY DOUGH: They were shooting Wiener warning glances to stay back at least a hundred feet.

WIENER: No, they were inviting me in, I can tell.

TOTLE: You're gonna go inside her eye?

DOVER: I think she has contacts.

PLAY DOUGH: I'm sure Melman would ever like you.

WIENER: Wanna bet?

PLAY DOUGH: Yeah, I'll bet you a million canteen tickets.

WIENER: Make it a billion.

STEINBERG: Guys, I've done the math. The max earning potential is 247 canteen tickets per summer.

PLAY DOUGH: Fine. 247. You see what I have to deal with here, new kid?

SMELLY: It's Robert. But you can call me Bobby.

WIENER: Yo— Play Dough! Did you hear this kid's name?

PLAY DOUGH: Yeah— Robert slash Bobby. We all heard it, brain-clog.

STEINBERG: But... I'm Robert slash Bobby at home.

TOTLE: Well, what's your last name?

SMELLY: Benjamin.

DOVER: But my first name is Benjamin!

PLAY DOUGH: Yeah, we can't have that. You're gonna need a nickname.

SMELLY: What?

SONG #2: NICKNAME

STEINBERG:
MY PARENTS CALL ME ROBERT
I'M A LONELY ONLY CHILD
AND I'M REALLY GOOD AT SCIENCE
BUT I'M BAD AT MAKING FRIENDS

STEINBERG (CONT'D):
WELL MOM AND DAD GOT WORRIED
HOW COULD NO ONE LOVE THEIR ROBERT?
SO THEY SIGNED ME UP FOR SUMMER CAMP
AND LOADED UP THE BENZ.
BUT ROBERT NEVER WAS A NAME
THAT EVER GOT ME VERY FAR
SO I SAID, "HEY, CALL ME STEINBERG!"
TOTLE:
AND I SAID, "HEY! NICE CAR!"
STEINBERG:
YOU GOTTA HAVE A NICKNAME.
PLAY DOUGH, STEINBERG, WIENER, TOTLE & DOVER:
YOU GOT TO HAVE A NICKNAME
'CAUSE WHEN YOU HAVE A NICKNAME
YOU CAN REALLY MAKE A NAME.

Music vamps under dialogue.

DOVER: That's not a nickname, it's just your last name.

PLAY DOUGH: Dude, your nickname is your last name.

DOVER: Touché.

SMELLY: Your name is Ben Dover?

DOVER: Yup.

SMELLY: No way! What about you, Play Dough?

PLAY DOUGH:
AT SCHOOL I'M KNOWN AS BRIAN
MESSY LOSER BRIAN GARFINK
I GET PAID TO RUN ON TREADMILLS

WIENER: Who pays you, your mom?

PLAY DOUGH: Uh, yeah.

(Singing)
'CAUSE I LIKE TO EAT. A LOT.

STEINBERG: You should see him go. Remember when he ate that egg salad sandwich his mom made him for the first day of camp?

PLAY DOUGH: The flavor really kicks in after a week or so.

SMELLY: Ewwww.

PLAY DOUGH:
SO ONE DAY I GOT A PACKAGE
FILLED WITH PLAY DOUGH STUFFED IN BAGGIES
AND I WAS REALLY HUNGRY

PLAY DOUGH (CONT'D):
SO I ATE IT ON THE SPOT.
BUT THEN I STARTED FEELING SICK
SO I WENT RUNNING FOR THE CAN
AND I KINDA MADE A RAINBOW
SO THAT'S HOW IT ALL BEGAN.

SMELLY: I might throw up.

DOVER, PLAY DOUGH, STEINBERG, TOTLE & WIENER:
YOU GOTTA HAVE A NICKNAME
YOU GOT TO HAVE A NICKNAME
'CAUSE WHEN YOU HAVE A NICKNAME
YOU CAN REALLY MAKE A NAME

SMELLY: So, what about you, Totle? Where did your name come from?

TOTLE: All men by nature desire to know.

SMELLY: Huh?

TOTLE:
MY GIVEN NAME IS JUSTIN
I WAS NAMED FOR MY GREAT UNCLE
AND I'M KIND OF PHILOSOPHIC

STEINBERG: You mean philosophical.

TOTLE: Whatever.

(Singing)
BUT MY NAME'S A BIT TOO PLAIN
SO AT FIRST THEY TRIED OUT PLATO

PLAY DOUGH:
BUT THAT WAS TOO CONFUSING

STEINBERG:
AND SOCRATES WAS ALSO NIXED
'CAUSE THAT WAS TOO ARCANE

TOTLE:
BUT ARISTOTLE SORT OF FIT

PLAY DOUGH:
THOUGH IT WAS KINDA HARD TO SAY

PLAY DOUGH & STEINBERG:
SO WE SHORTENED IT TO TOTLE

TOTLE:
AND THAT'S WHO I AM TODAY

DOVER, PLAY DOUGH, STEINBERG, TOTLE & WIENER:
YOU GOTTA HAVE A NICKNAME
YOU GOT TO HAVE A NICKNAME

DOVER, PLAY DOUGH, STEINBERG, TOTLE & WIENE (CONT'D):
'CAUSE WHEN YOU HAVE A NICKNAME
YOU CAN REALLY MAKE A NAME

SMELLY: Okay, so we have Steinberg, Dover, Play Dough, and Totle. I'm afraid to ask, but where did Wiener—?

WIENER:
MY NAME IS ERNEST MEYER

TOTLE:
YEAH, HIS NAME IS REALLY ERNEST

WIENER: So...?

DOVER:
WANTED US TO CALL HIM ERNIE
SO OF COURSE WE CALLED HIM BERT.

PLAY DOUGH:
TURNED OUT BERT WAS REALLY GROUCHY
SO INSTEAD WE CALLED HIM OSCAR

DOVER & TOTLE:
AND SINCE HE HAD THE NAME ALREADY
OSCAR MEYER SEEMED TO WORK.

WIENER:
BUT STILL MY NICKNAME WASN'T RIGHT

PLAY DOUGH:
UNTIL WE HAD A STROKE OF LUCK

DOVER, PLAY DOUGH, STEINBERG & TOTLE:
THEN WE SIMPLY CALLED HIM WIENER

WIENER:
AND THAT ONE FINALLY STUCK

DOVER, PLAY DOUGH, STEINBERG, TOTLE & WIENER:
YOU GOTTA HAVE A NICKNAME
YOU GOT TO HAVE A NICKNAME
'CAUSE WHEN YOU HAVE A NICKNAME
YOU CAN REALLY MAKE A NAME.

Music vamps under dialogue.

PLAY DOUGH: All right, "New Bobby," what's your middle name?

SMELLY: Ernest.

WIENER: Ha! Ernest! No way!

TOTLE: Okay, people, we need some plan B inspiration.

DOVER: Do you have any savvy skills?

STEINBERG: Quirky hobbies?

WIENER: Go-to movie quotes?

TOTLE: Go-to normal quotes that like people say?

DOVER: What's your favorite tool in the toolbox?

TOTLE: Do you have a spirit animal?

PLAY DOUGH: Where are you from?

SMELLY: Well... I'm from New Jersey.

DOVER: New Jersey? I've been there. It smells funny.

PLAY DOUGH: Do you smell funny?

STEINBERG: Hey! That's it! Smelly!

WIENER: Smelly?

PLAY DOUGH: Smelly!

DOVER, PLAY DOUGH, STEINBERG, TOTLE & WIENER: Smelly!!

> *PLAY DOUGH picks up a broomstick and pushes SMELLY into a kneel.*

PLAY DOUGH: Kneel, Robert of Jersey... arise, SIR SMELLY!

> *PLAY DOUGH "knights" SMELLY with the broomstick.*

SMELLY: Guys, I really don't—

DOVER, PLAY DOUGH, STEINBERG, TOTLE & WIENER: SMELLY!!!!
> *(Singing)*
YOU GOTTA HAVE A NICKNAME

SMELLY: Does it have to be Smelly?

DOVER, PLAY DOUGH, STEINBERG, TOTLE & WIENER:
YOU GOT TO HAVE A NICKNAME

SMELLY: But I like my real name.

PLAY DOUGH, STEINBERG & WIENER:
'CAUSE WHEN YOU HAVE A NICKNAME
YOU CAN REALLY MAKE A NAME

SMELLY: Let's talk about this. We can come up with something better, can't we? How about Jersey?

DOVER, PLAY DOUGH, STEINBERG, TOTLE & WIENER:
WHEN YOUR NAME IS ROBERT
ROBERT'S ALL THAT YOU CAN BE

SMELLY: I'm totally cool with the limitations of Robert.

DOVER, PLAY DOUGH, STEINBERG, TOTLE & WIENER:
BUT WITH A NAME LIKE SMELLY
YOU CAN LEAVE A LEGACY!

SMELLY: I hate camp!

DOVER, PLAY DOUGH, STEINBERG, TOTLE & WIENER: Smelly!!!

SCENE 3

THE SUPPLY CLOSET

A small space with sports equipment, cleaning supplies, and all manner of camp "stuff" piled high on shelves on all sides. RICK and SARA enter.

SARA: What exactly are we getting in here?

RICK: I don't know, El Capitan said we have to do icebreaker games. Ooh, marshmallows. Perfect.

SARA: Perfectly stupid.

RICK: Oh, come on. It's hilarious.

SARA: It's stupid. Icebreaker games are stupid.

RICK: Why?

SARA: Because they all know each other! My girls have been at camp every summer since they were eight. The ice is broken, I promise you. Ugh, I can't believe it's only the first day, it feels like forever.

RICK: I love how camp kind of moves turtle slow for the first couple of weeks. Makes it last 'cause we all know once Visiting Day comes the summer flies.

SARA: Well, I look forward to the flying part.

RICK: Come on, Sara, this is what, your eighth summer?

SARA: Tenth.

RICK: Okay, yeah, right! So...

SARA: What?

RICK: Why are you so debbie downer on this summer, then? You love it here, I know you do!

SARA: Rick, just— leave me alone, okay?

RICK: That'll be kind of hard. We're age group co-counselors. Is it because of Todd?

SARA: What? No. I don't want to talk about it. Would you leave me alone? Is that so hard to do?

RICK: Uh, actually, kind of, since we're age group co-counselors—

SARA: I'm feeling really claustrophobic in here, can you—?

RICK: Yeah, sorry. See you tonight!

SARA exits. RICK waits a second, then follows.

SCENE 4

OUTSIDE

As the lights come up, the BOYS and GIRLS are finishing a three-legged race. They are paired up boy-girl. SLIMEY with SMELLY, MELMAN with WIENER, JAMIE with PLAY DOUGH, JENNY with TOTLE, SOPHIE with STEINBERG, and MISSI with DOVER.

The race ends. MELMAN and WIENER are the winners. STEINBERG puffs his inhaler.

MELMAN: Told you you were all going down! Yeah!

> *MELMAN high-fives WIENER. He goes a step further and puts his arm around her. She promptly tosses his arm off.*

RICK: Okay, time for the final game of the night. Before we get started, I want you to turn to your partner and tell each other one random thing about yourself. On your mark, get set—

JENNY: Do I have to stay with him?

SARA *(overlapping with Rick)*: No.

RICK *(overlapping with Sara)*: Yes.

TOTLE: "A true friend is one soul in two bodies."

JENNY: Ew.

JAMIE: You're like really smart.

SOPHIE: Did you just quote Aristotle? Soulmate.

JAMIE: Calm down, Sophie, they're just words. But, omigod, Jenny, I'll totally trade you Play Dough.

PLAY DOUGH: Hey!

JENNY: Omigod, you're the bestest friend ever!

STEINBERG: Bestest isn't a word.

JAMIE & JENNY: Bestest best!

> *Focus shifts to SLIMEY and SMELLY.*

SLIMEY *(to Smelly)*: I'm Slimey.

SMELLY: Is that a nickname?

SLIMEY: Well yeah, that's what everyone calls me.

SMELLY: But you're not slimy at all! You can get them to call you anything, like, uh, cool... cat or something.

SLIMEY: I like Slimey. When I was like eight I was a little dyslexic but not really and my grandparents used to call me "Smiley" in their letters. So when I wrote back, I signed off "love, Slimey" instead of "Smiley" and it was funny and it stuck. So, what's your real name, Smelly?

SMELLY: Wow, word travels fast. It's Robert. They're calling me Smelly but I wish they'd just call me Bobby.

SLIMEY: Okay, Bobby.

RICK interrupts.

RICK: Alright, now that you've learned some random info, let's move on to a Camp Rolling Hills favorite. Each pair is going to get one of these marshmallows on a licorice string.

PLAY DOUGH: Sweetsauce!

RICK: Do not eat the marshmallow.

PLAY DOUGH: Soursauce!

RICK: Each partner is going to take an end of the string and put it in their mouth. When I say go, you start eating. Whoever gets to the marshmallow first wins!

WIENER: Best. Game. Ever.

MISSI: This is totally awk.

JAMIE & JENNY: We like have braces.

SARA: That's never stopped you girls from eating candy before.

SOPHIE: I'm allergic to red dye.

MELMAN: You ate a Fruit Roll-Up during rest hour.

SARA: I have Epi in ready-to-stab position, you're fine.

RICK: It looks like everyone's... good. On your mark, get set, go!

> *They race each other to the center. MELMAN easily beats WIENER.*

MELMAN: Ha! Sucker!

WIENER: This was actually a really good experience for me.

> *PLAY DOUGH yanks the whole thing away from JENNY and stuffs it in his mouth.*

JENNY: Ew, no fair!

> *TOTLE beats JAMIE, MISSI beats DOVER, STEINBERG beats SOPHIE, and SLIMEY beats SMELLY. Focus shifts to Slimey and Smelly.*

SLIMEY: Yes! I win! Want a bite?

SMELLY: Uh, it was already in your mouth.

SLIMEY: It's camp. We share everything.

SMELLY: That's... weird.

RICK: Alright! Good job, everybody. Hug it out.

SARA: Or... skip the hugs and line up: boys over there, girls with me.

The campers mill around, continue to chat, and finally get into two distinct lines throughout this scene. They can even start to leave.

SLIMEY: So, um, how do you like camp so far?

SMELLY: It's fine.

SLIMEY: It's fun, you'll like it soon. The first time I came here it took me a couple of days to realize how much I loved it but once you do you love it forever.

SMELLY: It doesn't matter. I won't be here next summer. My parents told me I could go back to baseball camp.

SLIMEY: Cool...

SMELLY: Yeah, I didn't want to come here but my parents are separating and they needed the eight weeks to sort stuff out. Baseball camp's only three.

SLIMEY: Oh. I'm sorry. About your parents, I mean.

SMELLY: Yeah, well...

SLIMEY: Look, if it makes you feel any better, last summer Jamie's parents got divorced and the year before that Missi's parents split up and neither of them ever wanted to go home.

SMELLY: Really? What about your parents, are they together?

SLIMEY: My dad's— yeah, it's like... Camp is weird. Sometimes it doesn't hit you till you're home at the end of the summer but then you're like, "Wow, that was amazing, I'm reverse homesick, I'm campsick" and then you can't stop thinking about it, you know? I'm not saying it's definitely gonna be like that for you, but maybe you'll like it better than baseball camp is all.

MELMAN: Slimey, let's go!

PLAY DOUGH: Come on, Smelly!

SLIMEY: I'm coming! Anyway, see you tomorrow, Bobby.

SMELLY: Bye.

They exit.

SCENE 5

GIRLS' CABIN (ANITA HILL CABIN)

SLIMEY and MELMAN are making their beds, decorating their areas, hanging posters, etc. JAMIE and JENNY sit in the middle of the room, playing an instinctively easy game of Jacks. MISSI watches them intently. In her top bunk, SOPHIE reads "Howling at the Sun, Part 2," highlighting her favorite parts.

MELMAN: The fact that they're calling him Smelly is a red flag.

SLIMEY: I didn't smell anything.

SOPHIE: I have allergy meds if you're feeling the aftermath.

SLIMEY: No, thanks.

MELMAN: Well, he sounds kinda weirdsauce.

SLIMEY: He's not... weirdsauce. He's nice.

JENNY: Omigod, do you like him?

JAMIE: Omigod yeah, Slimey, do you want to go out with him?

MISSI *(awkwardly)*: Omigod yeah...

SLIMEY: What? No. I mean, I just met him.

MISSI *(pointing to her cat poster)*: There is such a thing as love at first sight.

MELMAN: Did you just compare Smelly to a cat?

MISSI: He wishes.

JENNY: Well, if you don't like him then can Jamie ask him out?

SLIMEY: Yeah, whatever. Who cares?

JENNY: Omigod, hotsauce.

> *JAMIE and JENNY move to the top of their bunk bed and whisper. MISSI attempts to be part of the conversation and fails.*

MELMAN: Oh, Slimes, I'm really glad you came back. I don't think I could handle the J-squad without you.

SLIMEY: Of course I came back. Why wouldn't I?

MELMAN: I don't know. Bad memories?

> *SLIMEY takes out a locket on a gold chain. She hangs it on the underside of MELMAN's top bunk, so that it hangs down over her bottom bunk.*

SLIMEY: The bad memories are at home, too.

MELMAN: I know, but like, you found out he died right in the—

SLIMEY: I know where I found out, Melman. Being at home is worse. There's pictures of him and all his clothes are still in the closet, and my mom, you know, is...

> *She starts to choke up.*

MELMAN: Yeah.

SLIMEY: Here I have the locket he gave me and I have you. I'll be fine.

MELMAN: Together we'll make it the best summer ever, you'll see.

> *SLIMEY smiles at MELMAN. Focus shifts to JENNY and JAMIE.*

JENNY: Omigod, seriously Jamie, you have to do it.

JAMIE: What if he says no?

JENNY: He won't. We'll make a plan. Omigod, it'll be so much fun. He could be your Christopher.

JAMIE & JENNY (*sighing dreamily*): Christopher...

JAMIE: Have you heard from him yet?

JENNY: Omigod, yeah, he texted me before dinner (*She pulls out a cell phone, reading*) Miss ya. Smiley face.

JAMIE: Omigod, that is so cutesauce. You are so lucky your mom let you bring your celly.

> SARA comes out of her room, a glorified closet off the cabin.

SARA: Did someone say cell phone?

> JENNY scrambles to hide the cell phone in her cubby amongst her clothes. It doesn't fool SARA.

Jenny...

> JENNY hands her a cell phone.

I get fifty bucks for every one of these puppies I hand in to the Captain. So, I will find ALL of them. And I will read your texts over the PA, dramatize those emoticons so hard you'll be wishing cell phones were never invented. Anyone else? (*Pause*) Lights out in 10.

> She exits.

MELMAN: What's up her butt?

MISSI: You wanna know?

JAMIE: What's up her butt? Ew, no.

MISSI: Sara's just mad because she only came back for Todd Bergman who was supposed to come back but then he dumped her AND didn't come back.

MELMAN, SLIMEY & SOPHIE: Ouch.

MISSI: My sister told me, you know, 'cause she and Todd's sister are totally BFF.

JAMIE: Omigod, Jenny, I'm so sorry about your phone.

JENNY (*loudly, for Sara to hear*): Omigod, it's fine, I totally deserved it. (*Whispering*) I gave her my fake. I hid the real one in my cubby.

JAMIE: Omigod, you are a genius!

JENNY: Shh.

JAMIE (*whispering*): You're a genius.

JENNY: It was my mom's idea. So, what should I say back to him?

JAMIE: LOL?

MISSI: What exactly would she be laughing out loud about?

JAMIE: I don't know, your face?

MISSI: Isn't my face like irrelevant to the conversation?

JENNY: Focus, Jamie. This is why we need to get you a boyfriend stat.

JAMIE: I know, but I just don't like anyone right now.

JENNY: You just said you were totally into the new kid.

JAMIE: I did?

JENNY: Why are you blocking your emotions so early in the relationship?

JAMIE: I don't know... maybe I'm scared.

JENNY: There's no need to be scared. Having a boyfriend is amazing.

SONG #3: BOYFRIEND

(Singing)
DON'T YOU SEE
THAT IF WE BOTH HAD BOYFRIENDS WE COULD BE
LIKE SUPER TIGHT
'CAUSE WE COULD TALK ABOUT THEM EVERY NIGHT
AND I COULD SAY
HOW HANDSOME CHRISTOPHER HAD LOOKED THAT DAY
THEN I'D ASK YOU
AND YOU'D SAY "MINE LOOKED REALLY HANDSOME TOO"
THAT'S WHAT IT'D BE LIKE
IF I GOT YOU A BOYFRIEND

JAMIE:
OH MY GOD
IF THERE WERE FOUR OF US WE'D MAKE A QUAD
AND THAT'D BE COOL
'CAUSE WE COULD ALL HANG OUT LIKE AFTER SCHOOL
AND WHILE WE'RE HERE
LIKE YOU CAN HELP ME OVERCOME MY FEAR
'CAUSE I AGREE
BUT I'M AFRAID THERE'S NO ONE HERE FOR ME
AT LEAST NO ONE PERFECT
BUT I WANT A BOYFRIEND

JAMIE & JENNY:
WOULDN'T IT BE GREAT
IF WE COULD EVEN BE TOGETHER ON A DOUBLE-DATE
THIS IS WHAT YOU REALLY NEED
BUT I DON'T WANT TO LET YOU DOWN
AND THAT IS WHY I MUST SUCCEED
SO I'M GONNA FIND YOU/ME A BOYFRIEND

MELMAN: Stop!

>   (Singing)
>   WHAT A JOKE
>   THIS CONVERSATION MAKES ME WANT TO CHOKE
>   YOU'LL BE JUST FINE
>   YOU'LL GET A BOYFRIEND SOMEWHERE DOWN THE LINE
>   THOUGH I DON'T KNOW WHY
>   I MEAN YOU CAN SURVIVE WITHOUT A GUY
>   AND IN THE END
>   YOU GUYS ARE STILL EACH OTHER'S CLOSEST FRIEND
>   GET IT TOGETHER
>   YOU DON'T NEED A BOYFRIEND

JENNY: We never said we need one, but like it would be so much better if we did.

SLIMEY: Maybe... but I think you're going after a boyfriend for the wrong reasons.

JAMIE: Why is it wrong to like want to be loved?

MELMAN: That's not at all (what I meant)...

SLIMEY: What I'm saying is don't just want a boyfriend so you can talk about them together and double-date. It's more than that.

>   (Singing)
>   IT COULD BE SO NICE
>   TO HAVE A GUY WHO I COULD TALK TO WHEN I NEED ADVICE
>   DON'T YOU THINK IT WOULD BE SWEET
>   TO BE WITH SOMEONE SO FANTASTIC
>   HE COULD MAKE ME FEEL COMPLETE
>   THAT'S WHY YOU SHOULD WANT A BOYFRIEND

MISSI: You're right, Slimey. That's totally it!

>   (Singing)
>   COMMON GROUND
>   CAN SPARK A ROMANCE LIKE YOU'VE NEVER FOUND

SOPHIE:
>   I AGREE
>   LIKE IF YOU BOTH LIKE VAMPIRES THAT IS KEY

MISSI:
>   IT WOULD BE SO CUTE
>   LIKE IF MY BOYFRIEND ALSO PLAYED THE FLUTE

SOPHIE:
>   YOU COULD HARMONIZE

MISSI:
  AND WE COULD GAZE INTO EACH OTHER'S EYES

MISSI & SOPHIE:
  THAT SOUNDS AMAZING
  NOW I WANT A BOYFRIEND

MELMAN: What? You guys too?

SOPHIE: Come on, don't tell me you never want a relationship.

MISSI: Like, what if he played soccer?

MELMAN: Well, maybe eventually...

GIRLS:
  WOUNLDN'T IT BE GRAND
  TO HAVE A BOYFRIEND WHO WOULD DANCE WITH ME
  AND HOLD MY HAND
  HE WOULD MAKE ME LAUGH A LOT
  AND HE'D ALWAYS CALL ME PRETTY
  EVEN WHEN I'M REALLY NOT

SARA (*emerging from her room, cutting them off*): Yeah, I get it, boyfriends are totally awesome. That is until they tell you they're coming back to camp to be with you and then break your heart and stomp on it with their lies and perfect hair and strong calf muscles from running track...

  All music stops. Then, after a brief pause, MELMAN sings.

MELMAN:
  SEE YOU DON'T NEED A BOYFRIEND

JAMIE:
  BUT I WANT A BOYFRIEND

MISSI & SOPHIE:
  AND I REALLY WANT A BOYFRIEND

SLIMEY:
  AND I WANT—

GIRLS:
  I WANT
  A BOYFRIEND!

SCENE 6

BOYS CABIN (SAN JUAN HILL CABIN)

A few nights later. The cabin is dark and quiet except for a few faint strums of a guitar, coming from RICK, outside. SMELLY tosses and turns in his bed. Then he gives up, climbs down and goes outside.

RICK is idly plucking the guitar when SMELLY startles him.

RICK: Oh, hey buddy. How's it going?

SMELLY: I can't sleep.

RICK: You try reading or writing a letter or something?

SMELLY: You said lights out. Can I just sit outside with you for a minute until I get tired?

RICK: It's cool. But if Caperooski comes by, you gotta jet inside, okay?

SMELLY sits down next to RICK.

SMELLY: Practicing?

RICK: Eh, just playin' around. You into music?

SMELLY: Yeah. I have three thousand songs on my iPod. Well, it's my dad's old one but he gave it to me.

RICK: Cool, what's your favorite band?

SMELLY: I don't know. The Beatles, I guess. Eric Clapton.

RICK: Sweet, Clapton's the man. You a Phish fan?

SMELLY: My mom makes good tuna.

RICK: Okay, baby steps. You ever play before?

SMELLY: Nah.

RICK: You know, if you're really into music, I bet with some practice you could be good at this.

SMELLY: Like good-good?

RICK: Yeah, like good-good.

SMELLY: I dunno, I'm not really good at anything.

SONG #4: EVERYBODY'S GOOD AT SOMETHING

RICK:
> EVERYBODY'S GOOD AT SOMETHING

SMELLY: Everybody's good at something?

RICK:
> YES EVERYBODY HAS A TALENT
> THAT THEY WERE ALWAYS MEANT TO SHARE
> AND NOTHING ELSE CAN QUITE COMPARE
> TO FINDING OUT JUST WHAT YOUR GIFT MIGHT BE
>
> I'M NOT GOOD AT FOLLOWING DIRECTIONS
> SO I DON'T REALLY DO TOO WELL IN SCHOOL

RICK (CONT'D):
> BUT EVERY SUMMER HERE
> I'M COUNSELOR OF THE YEAR
> AND THEN MY GRADES DON'T MATTER MUCH TO ME
>
> 'CAUSE EVERYBODY'S GOOD AT SOMETHING

SMELLY:
> EVERYBODY'S GOOD AT SOMETHING

RICK:
> YES EVERYBODY'S BORN FOR SOMETHING
> LIKE I WAS BORN TO MAKE CAMP FUN
> THERE'S SOMETHING GREAT IN EVERYONE
> SO THERE'S PROBABLY SOMETHING REALLY GREAT IN YOU

SMELLY:
> WELL ONCE I GOT A HUNDRED ON A MATH TEST

RICK: Eh, keep going.

SMELLY:
> AND ONCE I BATTED IN THE WINNING RUN

RICK: Alright, that's something.

SMELLY:
> I'M NOT TOO BAD AT CHESS
> I NEVER LEAVE A MESS
> AND ONE TIME SOMEONE TOLD ME I COULD SING

RICK: Yeah, you're pretty good!

> *(Singing)*
> 'CAUSE EVERYBODY'S GOOD AT SOMETHING

SMELLY:
> EVERYBODY'S GOOD AT SOMETHING

RICK:
> YES EVERYBODY'S GOOD AT SOMETHING
> SO TRY WHATEVER COMES YOUR WAY
> 'CAUSE THIS COULD BE YOUR LUCKY DAY
> WHEN YOU FIND OUT YOU'RE GOOD AT SOMETHING TOO

RICK: Here. I'm gonna teach you a chord.

> *RICK hands his guitar to SMELLY.*

Ready?

SMELLY: I guess, sure.

RICK: Alright, here we go. You put this finger here on the top string, then this one a little further down between the second and third fret. These are called frets. And then, the ring finger goes down here on the bottom string. Good?

RICK (CONT'D): Okay, now strum.

> *He does.*

And that, my friend, is a G Chord.

> *SMELLY strums it a few more times.*

SMELLY: Cool! Can you teach me more?

RICK: Absolutely. Hey, I've got an idea. How about I teach you to play a song for Campstock— the talent show?

SMELLY: Cool! But—

RICK: At least give it a try— that's what camp's all about.

SMELLY: Okay.

RICK: Yeah?

SMELLY: I'll do it.

> *(Singing)*
> 'CAUSE EVERYBODY'S GOOD AT SOMETHING

RICK:
> YES EVERYBODY'S GOOD AT SOMETHING

SMELLY:
> EVERYBODY'S GOOD AT SOMETHING

RICK:
> AND ONCE YOU LEARN TO PLAY GUITAR
> I KNOW YOU'LL FEEL LIKE YOU'RE A STAR

SMELLY:
> 'CAUSE EVERYBODY'S GOOD AT SOMETHING

RICK:
> EVERYBODY'S GOOD AT SOMETHING

SMELLY:
> YES EVERYBODY'S BORN FOR SOMETHING
> LIKE I WAS BORN TO STRUM THE STRINGS

RICK:
> AND MAYBE THERE ARE LOTS OF OTHER THINGS
> THAT YOU COULD DO THAT MAKE YOU WHO YOU ARE

SMELLY:
> THAT I COULD DO THAT MAKE ME WHO I AM
> *(Speaking)*

Thanks, Rick.

> *RICK leads SMELLY in a camp handshake. As they pound, he undercuts Smelly's fist with a peace sign, together making what looks like a snail!*

SCENE 7

SPLIT SCENE: ANITA HILL CABIN / SAN JUAN HILL CABIN

TJ and CAPTAIN converse over the PA while the BOYS and GIRLS make their way into their respective cabins.

TJ: Good morning, Camp Rolling Hills! Mr. Sun is really making his golden presence known today. No camper is gonna want to be stuck inside cleaning the cabin on a day like this!

CAPTAIN: Actually, it's very important that the cabins are clean. Inspection will be in 20 minutes. And be sure to write a letter home. Especially you, Robert Steinberg. Your mother has called me seven times this week, asking how you're doing. She's driving me bananas—

TJ: —are filled with potassium!

PA goes off with a sharp squeal.

Focus on Anita Hill Cabin. The GIRLS check the job chart. The jobs correlate to the shower order of the evening: worst job = first shower.

JAMIE: Ugh, I'm sweeper!

JENNY: Ugh, I'm dustpan!

SOPHIE: Yes, I'm bathroom!

MISSI: Why are you happy to be bathroom?

SOPHIE: Worst job gets first shower, duh.

The GIRLS start to clean. JAMIE lip syncs into the broomstick.

MELMAN: Hey, Slimey, can I borrow a piece of paper?

SLIMEY: Sure.

MELMAN: And a pen?

SLIMEY: Yeah.

MELMAN: And an envelope?

SLIMEY: Okay.

MELMAN: And a stamp?

SLIMEY: Really?

Focus shifts to San Juan Hill Cabin: BOYS do anything but clean. They lay around, jump on their beds, wrestle. PLAY DOUGH eats a Slim Jim he's hidden in his socks. SMELLY plucks at RICK's guitar.

SONG #5: LETTER WRITING

Music up. RICK enters.

RICK: What's going on, guys? You're supposed to be cleaning up! Then writing letters! Gimme the guitar, slowhand. We're not going anywhere until I have a letter from every one of you punks. Especially you, Steinberg.

STEINBERG: I gotta change my shirt first.

> *Vamp under dialogue.*
>
> *STEINBERG changes his shirt throughout the song. By the end, he should have an accumulated pile of shirts. Meanwhile, TOTLE collects his cabinmates' clothes from the floor. He evaluates each item with a quick sniff and throws the "clean" clothes in an empty cubby, the "dirty" clothes in a laundry bin. Each time he makes the shot, he marks the wall with chalk.*

PLAY DOUGH: Dear Mom...

> *(Singing)*
> THIS SUMMER THE FOOD IS
> MUCH WORSE THAN IT WAS LAST YEAR
> THE FRENCH FRIES ARE SOGGY
> AND THEY ONLY HAVE PURPLE PUNCH
> AND TOO MANY TIMES
> THERE JUST ISN'T ENOUGH TO EAT
> AND THREE TIMES THIS WEEK
> WE HAD TUNA FISH FOR LUNCH

> *Focus shifts to Anita Hill Cabin.*

SLIMEY: Dear Mom— let's see, where did I leave off—? So much has happened since my last letter I don't know if I'll be able to fit it all in. When I woke up this morning, my counselor Sara didn't have to threaten me with a water gun to get me out of bed. I just got up. I think it's because I am in the middle of four arts & crafts projects and I can't wait to finish them.

JENNY:
> DEAR CHRISTOPHER
> HOW ARE YOU?
> I'M FINE
> I'M HAVING AN AWESOME TIME
> I MISS YOU EVERY DAY
> I REALLY REALLY MISS YOU.
> HOW'S THE LAKE?
> DID YOUR DAD LET YOU DRIVE THE JETSKI?
> I HOPE SO 'CAUSE THAT'D BE COOL.

MELMAN: Hey Slimey!
> *(Singing)*
> HOW DO YOU SPELL MASSACHUSETTS

SLIMEY:
WHY DO YOU NEED TO SPELL MASSACHUSETTS?
MELMAN:
I HAVE A FRIEND WHO MOVED TO MASSACHUSETTS.
SLIMEY:
OH! IT'S M-A-S-S-A-C-H-U-S-E-T-T-S.
MELMAN: Thanks!

Focus shifts to San Juan Cabin.

PLAY DOUGH:
PLEASE SEND ME A PACKAGE
WITH PRINGLES POTATO CHIPS
AND PRETZELS AND POP TARTS
AND THAT SQUEEZY E-Z CHEEZ!
OR SOMETHING MORE HEALTHY
LIKE KUDOS GRANOLA BARS
AND A THREE GALLON BAG OF
REESE'S PEANUT BUTTER CUPS.

WIENER crams the following information onto a postcard.

WIENER: Dear Little Bro— Camp keeps getting better and better. To say I'm popular is an understatement. Everything I do becomes a tradition. Like, all my catchphrases make camp history.

SMELLY writes two letters simultaneously; one to his mom (M), and one to his dad (D).

SMELLY:
DEAR MOM (M)
DEAR DAD (D)
CAMP IS NOT SO BAD (M)
CAMP IS NOT SO BAD (D)
I'M LEARNING THE GUITAR (M)
TODAY WE'RE PLAYING BASEBALL (D)
I'VE MADE A LOT OF FRIENDS (M)
MY COUNSELOR'S REALLY AWESOME (D)
I MET THIS GIRL NAMED SLIMEY (M)
I MISS YOU MOM, (M)
I MISS YOU DAD, (D)
I REALLY MISS THE FAMILY THAT WE HAD (M)

Focus shifts to Anita Hill Cabin.

SLIMEY: And everyone in my group is the same as last year. It's me and Missi and Sophie and Melman— you remember her, right? She's like my best friend here, the one who always wears a baseball hat— and Jamie and Jenny who are like, totally inseparable.

MISSI:
> DEAR GRANDMA
> GOT YOUR LETTER
> GOT YOUR DOLLAR
> THANKS A LOT!
> TELL GRANDPA
> THAT I'M SORRY
> 'BOUT HIS PROSTATE
> WHATEVER THAT... IS.

SOPHIE:
> DEAR GEORGINA WHITEFOOT
> I'M PSYCHED TO WRITE TO YOU
> I HAVE A MILLION QUESTIONS TO ASK
> 'BOUT HOWLING AT THE SUN (PART TWO)

MELMAN:
> HOW DO YOU SPELL CANOEING?

SLIMEY:
> WHY DO YOU NEED TO SPELL CANOEING?
> WE HAVEN'T EVEN GONE CANOEING.

MELMAN:
> I'M ASKING HER IF SHE WENT CANOEING.

SLIMEY:
> FINE! IT'S C-A-N-O-E-I-N-G.

Focus shifts to San Juan Hill Cabin.

WIENER: Even though I'm the youngest in my cabin, it's like I'm the oldest when we play sports. In Table Tennis, I bring out the ping in pong. That's just something the little kids say about me 'cause I'm their idol when it comes to athletics.

PLAY DOUGH:
> AND GUMMY BEARS
> AND GUMMY WORMS
> AND SOUR GUMMY WORMS
> AND FUNIONS AND SLIM JIMS
> AND A CAN OF MOUNTAIN DEW.
> AND CHEETOS, DORITOS, AND FRITOS AND STUFF LIKE THAT
> AND A BOTTLE OF GATORADE
> THE ORANGE OR THE BLUE.

DOVER: Dear Bethany...

> *(Singing)*
> MOM AND DAD SAID I HAD TO
> SO I'M WRITING TO YOU EVEN THOUGH YOU'RE STUPID

TOTLE: Dear Journal,
>   *(Singing)*
> TODAY I'LL KEEP IT NICE AND SHORT
> I FOUND A WAY TO TURN LAUNDRY INTO A SPORT

>> *Focus shifts to Anita Hill Cabin. JAMIE fills out a form postcard.*

JAMIE:
> DEAR BLANK

JENNY:
> WHO'S BLANK?

JAMIE:
> I KNOW! MY UNCLE FRANK!
> CAMP IS BLANK. TODAY WE BLANK.
>   *(Speaking)*

We didn't do anything today. It's morning.

JENNY: Omigod, say you woke up.

JAMIE:
> I'LL JUST LEAVE IT BLANK
> THE FOOD IS BLANK

JENNY:
> DETESTABLE!

JAMIE: Omigod, nice word!

JENNY: Thanks!

>> *Musical themes start to cross in and out. Focus is on both Anita Hill Cabin and San Juan Hill Cabin.*

SOPHIE:
> WHY DO VAMPIRES SPARKLE IN THE SUN?

MISSI:
> GOT YOUR POSTCARD
> THANKS A LOT!

MELMAN:
> HOW DO YOU SPELL SAN JUAN
>   *(Speaking)*

With a "W"?

PLAY DOUGH:
> AND CHOCOLATE AND NOUGAT
> AND GOOEY CARAMEL

JENNY:
> DID YOUR DAD LET YOU DRIVE THE SPEEDBOAT?

DOVER:
> YOU STINK!

JENNY:
I HOPE SO CUZ THAT'D BE COOL
PLAY DOUGH:
AND A BIG TURKEY SANDWICH
FROM THE DELI ON OUR STREET
JAMIE:
SINCERELY BLANK
SINCERELY JAMIE
TOTLE:
SINCERELY JUSTIN
WIENER:
LATER BUDDY WRITE BACK SOON, ERNIE
SLIMEY:
HAVE A GREAT SUMMER
MELMAN:
YOUR FRIEND
SMELLY:
YOUR SON
SOPHIE:
YOUR FAN
JENNY:
WITH LOVE
DOVER:
WITH HATE!
PLAY DOUGH:
SEND FOOD
MISSI:
I LOVE YA!

DOVER: Just kidding!

SLIMEY:
STEPHANIE
MISSI:
MELISSA
SMELLY:
ROBERT
MELMAN:
STACY
PLAY DOUGH:
BRIAN
SOPHIE:
SOPHIE
JENNY:
JENNY

DOVER:
> BEN

> *Focus shifts to San Juan Hill Cabin. RICK enters.*

RICK: Alright, hand em over. Steinberg, where's your letter?

STEINBERG: Um—

RICK: You had 20 minutes to write a letter. What were you doing?

STEINBERG: I had to change my shirt.

RICK: Nobody's going anywhere until Steinberg writes a letter.

> *RICK hands STEINBERG a postcard and a pen.*

DOVER, PLAY DOUGH & TOTLE *(ad lib)*: Come on, Steinberg, just do it already!

STEINBERG: Fine.

SONG #5A: STEINBERG'S LETTER

> *STEINBERG plops down on the pile of shirts he just made. He sings.*

> *(Singing)*
> DEAR MOM AND DAD
> I'M ALIVE
> CAMP'S GOOD
> LOVE, YOUR SON
> ROBERT.

> *He hands the postcard to RICK. RICK opens the door. All exit.*

SCENE 8

OUTSIDE

> *BOYS (except SMELLY) and GIRLS play Newcomb "battle of the sexes" style: boys on one side, girls on the other. SMELLY sits on the opposite end of the stage, his back to the action, listening to his iPod. JENNY and JAMIE are "out"— they stand on the sideline.*

JENNY: Play Dough! Get out, I have to talk to you.

PLAY DOUGH: What? No way. I'm playing until I—

> *MELMAN throws the ball over the net. It hits PLAY DOUGH in the head as he talks to JENNY. He's out!*

JENNY: Thanks, Melman.

MELMAN: Any time. Jamie, you're back in.

JAMIE: No, thanks!

> *PLAY DOUGH shuffles over to JENNY and JAMIE. The game continues as they talk.*

JENNY: So, does Smelly like Jamie?

JAMIE: Jenny!

PLAY DOUGH: Uh, I don't think so...?

JENNY: Why not?

PLAY DOUGH: Look at him. He's sitting over there by himself. If he was interested, he'd stare at her and like touch her hair.

JENNY: Is that what you think flirting looks like?

PLAY DOUGH: No. I dunno.

JENNY: You need to ask him.

JAMIE: Wait, but— but...

JENNY: Omigod, obviously he's not just gonna ask him like directly.

PLAY DOUGH: So... how am I supposed to...?

JENNY: You just have to ask him if he likes ANYONE. And if he's like shy about it be like, "Jamie's hot" so it's like in his subconscious when he dreams and stuff.

JAMIE: Oh yeah, I like that plan.

> *SLIMEY drops the ball.*

SLIMEY: Play Dough, you're back in. Hey, why isn't Bobby playing?

DOVER: Who? You mean, Steinberg?

STEINBERG: I'm right here, in front of your face.

SLIMEY: No, the other Bobby.

DOVER: She means Smelly.

SLIMEY: Yeah. Why is he sitting out?

WIENER: What do you care, Slimey? Do you like, like him?

MELMAN: Zip it, Wiener. No one wants to hear your voice.

PLAY DOUGH: You could just ask him yourself if you're so curious.

SLIMEY: Maybe I will.

PLAY DOUGH: Yeah, I'm sure you're gonna—

> *SLIMEY approaches SMELLY.*

> (Stunned)

Oh. Okay, good.

TOTLE: A challenge can be the greatest form of motivation.

SOPHIE: Swoon.

SLIMEY reaches SMELLY.

SLIMEY: Hey.

SMELLY's headphones prevent him from hearing SLIMEY. She waves a hand over his face.

Bobby, hey.

SMELLY takes his headphones out.

Hey, why aren't you playing?

SMELLY: Don't feel like it.

SLIMEY: Newcomb's fun if you wanna give it a shot. It's easy— I mean, you basically just throw and catch over the net.

SMELLY: It's not that, it's just—

MELMAN: Slimes, you're back in! Wiener can't catch!

WIENER *(running his hand through his hair)*: My hair gel gives me slippery fingers, if you must know.

MELMAN: Why are you wearing hair gel?

WIENER: To impress you!

MISSI: I love hair gel. I use it on my cat.

SLIMEY: Win it without me!

STEINBERG: Yes! Even teams! Way to go, Smelly!

SMELLY: You can play if you want, I don't wanna make you miss out...

SLIMEY: Nah, I'll play the next one.

Beat.

SMELLY: I got a letter from my dad, with a new address. He moved out.

SLIMEY: I'm sorry.

SMELLY: How could he just do that without telling me? Without asking me, or at least warning me, you know?

SLIMEY: Yeah.

SMELLY: I'm gonna kill him, I swear I will.

SLIMEY: Don't say that.

SMELLY: Why not?

SLIMEY: Because you don't mean it, trust me.

SMELLY: You don't get it, do you?

SLIMEY: I know you're hurt, Bobby, but look on the bright side.

SLIMEY (CONT'D):
>ONE TIME I WAS PAINTING A PICTURE
>FOR MY FINAL PROJECT IN ART
>IT WAS FROM A SEAGULL'S PERSPECTIVE
>FLYING TOWARD A HOT DOG CART
>I HAD BARELY FINISHED MY PICTURE
>WHEN MY DOG RAN IN FROM THE RAIN
>IT WAS NOT THE BEAGLE'S OBJECTIVE
>BUT HIS PAW PRINT LEFT A STAIN
>
>I GOT REALLY MAD
>AND I STARTED TO CRY
>TILL I NOTICED THAT HIS PAW PRINT
>COULD BE THE HOT DOG GUY
>AND SINCE IT SORTA FIT WITH MY STYLE
>I HAD A REASON TO SMILE

SMELLY: Look, I know you're just trying to help, but there's no bright side to divorce.

SLIMEY: Not if you don't look for it. Some things aren't meant to make you happy, but it doesn't mean you can't try to find a little happiness in them.
>*(Singing)*
>LAST YEAR I WAS PSYCHED FOR MY PARENTS
>TO COME UP FOR VISITING DAY
>I SPENT LOTS OF TIME GETTING READY
>ALL MY LANYARDS ON DISPLAY
>ALL MY FRIENDS HAD GONE TO THEIR PARENTS
>I WAS FORCED TO SIT THERE AND WAIT
>THEN MY COUNSELOR FOUND ME AND TOLD ME
>MINE WERE RUNNING KIND OF LATE
>
>I GOT REALLY SAD
>WONDERING WHERE COULD THEY BE
>TILL THE MELMANS CAME AND ASKED ME TO JOIN THEIR FAMILY
>AND EVEN THOUGH IT TOOK ME A WHILE
>I FOUND A REASON TO SMILE
>
>AND THOUGH THE DARKEST DAYS
>FEEL LIKE THE LONGEST BY FAR

SLIMEY (CONT'D):
> TOMORROW WILL BE BRIGHTER
> NO MATTER WHERE YOU ARE
>
> NOW I UNDERSTAND THAT YOU'RE ANGRY
> BUT BE GLAD YOU STILL HAVE A DAD
> THOUGH I'M SURE DIVORCE ISN'T EASY
> SOON YOU'LL SEE IT'S NOT SO BAD
>
> TRY TO RELAX
> THINK HOW GREAT IT COULD BE
> GETTING TWICE THE PRESENTS
> STACKED UP BENEATH YOUR CHRISTMAS TREE
> JUST THINK OF ALL THE STUFF IN THAT PILE
> AND YOU'LL HAVE A REASON TO SMILE
> THERE'S ALWAYS A REASON TO SMILE

SMELLY: Did your Dad...

SLIMEY: Die? Yeah. My mom was so— I mean she was a mess, and then my uncle— my mom's brother— came and took me home.

SMELLY: Are you okay?

SLIMEY: Kinda? There were times this year when I thought I might not be able to come back here again after everything. Not because my mom wouldn't let me or anything, but... I don't know. This place just makes me feel... better, and I know I made the right choice. And I have my locket my Dad gave me, so he's always with me. Except at Swim.

> *SLIMEY shows SMELLY the locket she's tucked under her shirt.*

SMELLY: I had no idea.

SLIMEY: Yeah. I liked that you didn't know. Talking to you about stuff without you like judging me or feeling bad for me— it was nice for a while. But now I'm glad I'm telling you.

SMELLY: I like talking to you for you, Slimey.

SLIMEY: Thanks.

SMELLY: You're the only person I've told about my dad. You won't tell anyone, right?

SLIMEY: Of course not. Your secret is safe with me.

SMELLY: Hey, come on, let's go play. Whoever wins has to buy the other a Butterfinger at Canteen tonight.

SLIMEY: Let's make it two.

> *SLIMEY smiles. SMELLY smiles.*

SMELLY: You're on!

> *They race to rejoin the game.*

SCENE 9

> *TJ and CAPTAIN converse over the PA.*

TJ: Hey, Captain, is there anything special happening tonight?

CAPTAIN: Why yes there is, TJ. *(Whispers)* One, two, three...

CAPTAIN & TJ: The Mid-Summer Dance!

CAPTAIN: While the girls get all dolled up...

TJ: The boys might shower.

CAPTAIN: Well, they have to shower. Boys, you have to shower.

TJ: And, I dunno, maybe tonight's the night you'll dance with that special someone.

CAPTAIN: Are you asking me to dance, TJ?

TJ: In a respectful, assertive, yet unaggressive way.

CAPTAIN: Oh well, that's just wonderful. I accept. And maybe you'll also be inclined to take me on a backstage tour after we've danced?

TJ: Sure.

CAPTAIN *(whispers):* No, that's not allowed, remember?

TJ: No, I will not take you there! 'Cause then I would...

CAPTAIN: Get held back from Canteen.

TJ: Really? That's not so bad.

CAPTAIN: For the whole summer!

TJ: Eek, that's rough. Everybody be sure to wear your dancing shoes, kick away those mid-summer blues.

CAPTAIN: If you've got 'em, which, hopefully you don't! And try to make note of at least three positive experiences tonight that you can perhaps include in a letter home tomorrow.

TJ: Your parents think we torture you.

CAPTAIN: Well, that's not—

> *PA goes off with a sharp squeal. PLAY DOUGH puts away fishing supplies, munches on bread. JENNY finds him.*

JENNY: Play Dough!

PLAY DOUGH: I'm putting them away! I'm putting them away, I swear! Oh, it's you.

JENNY: What are you doing?

PLAY DOUGH: Rick told me to put away the fishing rods and then meet back up with the group. But I got tired so I'm resting.

JENNY: And eating carbohydrates?

PLAY DOUGH: When I rest, I get hungry. Want some?

JENNY: Isn't that bread for the fish?

PLAY DOUGH: Only some of it was in the lake.

JENNY: Omigod, ew. I have to talk to you.

PLAY DOUGH: About what?

JENNY: Phase three.

PLAY DOUGH: What's phase three?

JENNY: Of the plan...

PLAY DOUGH: Oh, yeah, the plan.

SONG #7: BACKSTAGE

> *Music up.*

JENNY: And since, like, you failed at phase one and two and they were time sensitive, we're gonna have to move straight to phase three. We get Smelly to ask Jamie to dance at the dance.

PLAY DOUGH: Okay...

JENNY: And then, we get him to take her backstage.

> *(Singing)*
> WHEN A GIRL HAS A CRUSH ON A BOY
> AND THE BOY WANTS A GIRLFRIEND
> BUT DOESN'T KNOW WHO IT SHOULD BE
> SOMETIMES ALL THE WORK
> COMES DOWN TO PEOPLE LIKE YOU AND ME
> AND IF WE STICK TO THE PLAN THEY'LL BE ALONE
> AND THEY'LL BE FORCED TO ENGAGE
> WHEN WE TAKE THEM BACKSTAGE
> TAKE THEM BACKSTAGE

PLAY DOUGH: Backstage? Like backstage, backstage?

JENNY: No, backstage as in front of the stage where like everyone can see you.

> *(Singing)*
> WHEN THEY'RE STANDING ALONE IN THE DARK
> HE'LL HAVE NOTHING TO LOOK AT
> UNLESS HE LOOKS INTO HER EYES
> SHE'LL LOOK BACK AT HIM, THE SPARKS WILL FLY

JENNY (CONT'D):
> AND THAT'S NO SURPRISE
> AND WHEN AT LAST THEY COME OUT THEY'LL BE TOGETHER
> ON THE VERY SAME PAGE
> 'CAUSE WE GOT THEM BACKSTAGE
> GOT THEM BACKSTAGE

PLAY DOUGH: Okay, but I mean, how do you even get there? Is there a trap door or something?

JENNY: What? There's like a curtain.

PLAY DOUGH: Cool.

JENNY:
> SOME MIGHT SAY "TRY LOVER'S LANE
> IT'S SO ROMANTIC IN THE RAIN"

PLAY DOUGH:
> AT LEAST UNTIL YOU'RE FORCED TO RUN FOR COVER

JENNY & PLAY DOUGH:
> BEHIND THE CURTAIN IS THE ONLY PLACE YOU'RE CERTAIN
> TO SHOW HER THAT YOU LOVE HER
> YOU TAKE HER BACKSTAGE
> TAKE HER BACKSTAGE

PLAY DOUGH: Cool, cool. So, like, what exactly goes on back there? I mean, you said sparks fly, and I've heard stuff, and I mean, I know stuff too, but how am I... I mean, how are WE, going to get them to do it?

JENNY: Omigod, Play Dough, grow some faith in the plan.

Music continues under dialogue.

JAMIE *(from offstage)*: Jenny?

PLAY DOUGH: Wait, what am I supposed to do?

JENNY: Ugh, the plan! *(Shouting)* I'm over here!

JAMIE enters.

JAMIE: Omigod, I've been looking, like, everywhere for you.

JENNY: I have to tell you something.

JAMIE: Omigod, what is it? I'm scared.

JENNY: It's about the dance. And the plan. It's time for phase three.

JAMIE: Phase three?

JENNY whispers the plan into JAMIE's ear. JAMIE lets out a few "Omigod"s on rhythm as she listens.

JENNY:
> THEN YOU TAKE HIM BACKSTAGE

JAMIE & JENNY:
  TAKE HIM BACKSTAGE

SCENE 10 – CONTINUOUS

THE MID-SUMMER DANCE

The BOYS arrive! Music continues under the dialogue.

PLAY DOUGH: Yo. Smellsky.

SMELLY: Uh, yeah?

PLAY DOUGH: I know someone who likes you.

SMELLY: Cool. So do I.

PLAY DOUGH: You do?

SMELLY: Yeah.

PLAY DOUGH: Okay. Good. That was easy. *(Beat)* So are you gonna dance with her tonight?

SMELLY: I don't know. Maybe.

PLAY DOUGH: You've got to! This is like your chance of the summer. Listen…

          (Singing)
      SHE'LL BE STANDING ALONE OVER THERE
      SEE THAT LOOK ON HER FACE
      SHE WANTS YOU TO ASK HER TO DANCE
      POP A MENTOS IN YOUR MOUTH
      AND SHOW HER SOME TRUE ROMANCE
      GIRLS LIKE THEIR BOYS TO BE MEN
      SO JUST RELEASE YOUR INNER BEAST FROM ITS CAGE
      AND TAKE HER BACKSTAGE
      TAKE HER BACKSTAGE
JENNY & PLAY DOUGH:
      'CAUSE BACKSTAGE IS THE ONLY PLACE
      WHERE YOU CAN GET HER/HIM FACE TO FACE
      AND YOU MIGHT EVEN WANNA TRY TO KISS HER/HIM
      'CAUSE ONCE YOU'RE BACK THERE,
      YOU'RE ON THE RIGHT TRACK THERE
JENNY & PLAY DOUGH:
      YOU REALLY WOULDN'T WANT TO MISS HER/HIM
ALL CAMPERS EXCEPT SMELLY, SLIMEY & JAMIE:
      YOU TAKE HER/HIM BACKSTAGE
      TAKE HER/HIM BACKSTAGE

ALL CAMPERS EXCEPT SMELLY, SLIMEY & JAMIE (CONT'D):
TAKE HER/HIM BACKSTAGE
TAKE HER/HIM BACKSTAGE

SCENE 11 – CONTINUOUS

The Mid-Summer Dance is now in full swing. Pop re-mix of "Backstage" plays. STEINBERG is the DJ.

PLAY DOUGH: Dude-a-cris. It's almost time.

SMELLY: I don't know, what if she says no? What if she isn't ready?

PLAY DOUGH: She's ready. Listen, she wants to and Jenny's acting all crazy about it going down just as we planned, so you gotta do it.

SMELLY: I don't know... I don't wanna get in trouble.

PLAY DOUGH: Voilà!

PLAY DOUGH reveals a red cape from inside his pants.

SMELLY: What is that?

PLAY DOUGH: It's a disguise. I borrowed it from the costume closet. Wear this and no one will know who you are.

SMELLY: Maybe?

PLAY DOUGH: We all have your back. Do it for me. Do it for you. Do it for San Juan Hill!

SMELLY: Okay. Okay, I can do this!

PLAY DOUGH: Sauce!

PLAY DOUGH puts the cape on SMELLY.

Now, remember the signal?

SMELLY: When the slow song starts.

PLAY DOUGH: You got it. Alright, here we go...

Focus shifts to SOPHIE in STEINBERG's personal bubble as he DJs.

SOPHIE: Can you play "My Fangs Are Your Fangs"?

STEINBERG: Shouldn't you be dancing?

SOPHIE: I'm rather intimidated by the breakdancing happening at 2 o'clock.

Focus shifts to DOVER and TOTLE dancing.

DOVER: Sick move, Totle.

TOTLE *(doing the worm)*: No, man, I think a bug just went down my shirt.

DOVER: Smush it against your chest! Then eat it!

> *PLAY DOUGH crosses to the DJ booth. Focus shifts to SLIMEY and MELMAN dancing.*

SLIMEY: I can't believe you wore cleats to the Mid-Summer Dance.

MELMAN: Why? They elevate me like half an inch. I'm practically wearing heels.

SLIMEY: Don't you want the boys to ask you to dance?

MELMAN: Oh, don't worry, Slimes, one will.

> *Focus shifts to MISSI and WIENER.*

MISSI: Hey, Wiener, do you play a musical instrument?

WIENER: I dabble. Why? Do I come off as a prodigy or something?

MISSI: It's just your walk. Really nice rhythm.

WIENER: Oh, you mean my swagger?

> *WIENER swaggers on the dance floor with over-confidence.*

MISSI: Yeah! Yeah, like that!

> *Music changes.*

SONG #8: SLOW SONG

STEINBERG: Slow song!

> *WIENER swaggers over to MELMAN.*

WIENER: Hey Melman, wanna dance?

MELMAN: Why are you walking like that?

WIENER *(dropping the swagger):* Oh, I didn't notice.

MELMAN *(to Slimey):* See? *(To Wiener)* Alright, let's do this thing.

> *TJ and CAPTAIN grab the microphones. The campers and staff cheer, laugh, hoot, and holler as they sing. STEINBERG echoes TJ and Captain from the booth.*

TJ:
HOLD, HOLD ME TIGHT
HOLD ME CLOSE FOR THE REST OF THE NIGHT
DON'T YOU LET ME GO
I COULD STAY FOREVER HERE IN THIS MOMENT
THAT'S ALL I NEED TO KNOW

CAPTAIN:
SWAY IN MY ARMS
SOON ENOUGH YOU'LL SUCCUMB TO MY CHARMS
WE'LL GLIDE ACROSS THE FLOOR
EVERY STEP WE TAKE REMINDS ME I LOVE YOU
I COULDN'T LOVE YOU MORE

CAPTAIN & TJ:	(STEINBERG ECHOES):
AND THEY PLAY A SLOW SONG	(SLOW SONG!)
YOU CAN PLAY A SLOW SONG	(SLOW SONG!)
'CAUSE YOU JUST CAN'T GO WRONG	(GO WRONG)
WHEN YOU PLAY A SLOW SONG	(SLOW SONG!)
TWO HEARTS	(TWO HEARTS)
STAND AT LEAST TWO FEET APART	(FEET APART)
WHEN YOU PLAY A SLOW SONG	(SLOW SONG)
YOU CAN PLAY A SLOW SONG	YOU CAN PLAY A SLOW SONG

Music continues under dialogue.

JENNY: Okay, Jamie. Now.

JAMIE walks to where MELMAN was just standing, next to SLIMEY. She stops and strikes a strange, not-so-alluring pose.

SLIMEY: What are you doing?

JAMIE: Phase three. Omigod, here he comes.

SMELLY walks across the floor. JAMIE holds her pose and bats her eyes. Smelly ignores her, and instead addresses SLIMEY.

SMELLY: Hey, Slimey, will you dance with me?

JAMIE: Of course I— wait, whaaat?

JENNY: Whaaat? No! PLAY DOUGH!!

PLAY DOUGH: What's the—?

SLIMEY: Sure, I'll dance with you.

PLAY DOUGH: Oh. Oops.

SMELLY and SLIMEY dance. JENNY and PLAY DOUGH slow dance. JAMIE runs off to the side, buries her face in her hands.

TJ:
MY HANDS ON YOUR SHOULDERS, I LOOK YOU IN THE EYE
CAPTAIN:
NOTHING CAN KEEP ME FROM SMILING BACK AT YOU
TJ:
WE SWAY BACK AND FORTH AND I FEEL LIKE I CAN FLY

SOPHIE approaches TOTLE and just starts slow dancing. DOVER and MISSI gravitate toward each other by process of elimination.

CAPTAIN, TJ & STEINBERG:
AS LIFE BEGINS ANEW
BRIGHT AND ROMANTIC AND CHARMING AND ALL FOR YOU!

JAMIE wails.

CAPTAIN, TJ & STEINBERG (CONT'D):
INNOCENT GLANCING AND WILD ROMANCING
IT'S SO ENTRANCING
SLOW DANCING ALL OF MY WORRIES AWAY

TJ:
I HEAR WHAT YOU SAY AS YOU WHISPER IN MY EAR

CAPTAIN, TJ & STEINBERG:
AND I GAZE FOREVER
INTO YOUR EYES

> *SMELLY looks to PLAY DOUGH. Play Dough gives SMELLY a thumbs-up behind JENNY's back as he dances with her. Smelly interprets it as a signal to go ahead with taking SLIMEY backstage.*

SMELLY: Look, Slimey, would you like to, um, go backstage...

SLIMEY: I don't know if I'm ready for... backstage. I mean we're not even boyfriend and girlfriend yet.

SMELLY: Well, okay. Do you want to be boyfriend and girlfriend?

SLIMEY: Sure.

SMELLY: Good. So... then we can go backstage?

SLIMEY: I dunno, that's a big step, don't you think?

SMELLY: But, Play Dough said you were ready.

SLIMEY: Are you asking me or are you asking Play Dough?

SMELLY: You, of course! It's just that I like you, Slimey, and—

SLIMEY: I like you too. But, what's the rush?

SMELLY: Well, I think it's part of the plan... and this is our chance of the summer—

SLIMEY: What plan?

SMELLY: Phase three.

> *SLIMEY takes a step back.*

SLIMEY: I'm not part of a plan, Bobby! If we like each other, it's between us, not Play Dough or anyone else. I'm not like that, and I thought you weren't either.

> *PLAY DOUGH and JENNY gaze into each other's eyes for just a moment. It's broken by SLIMEY storming past them. Play Dough, overwhelmed by the intimacy, breaks from Jenny, and goes to SMELLY.*

PLAY DOUGH: What happened? You were so close!

SMELLY: What happened is you ruined it! It was none of your business, and I should have never listened to you!

SLIMEY *(passing Melman on the way out)*: You were right, Melman. *(Loud enough for Smelly to hear, referring to red cape)* Smelly is one giant red flag!

SMELLY *(calling to Slimey)*: What's that supposed to mean?

> *MELMAN follows SLIMEY out, leaving WIENER to dance alone.*

WIENER: Thanks a lot, Smelly. Do you have any idea how long I waited for this moment to arrive?

SMELLY: Blame Play Dough. He's the one who pushed me to do it!

> *JENNY follows SLIMEY and MELMAN out. SMELLY takes a seat on the other side, across from JAMIE.*

JAMIE *(to Jenny as she passes her)*: So you have to chase after Slimey to see if she's okay, but you have no problem humiliating and then leaving your best friend all alone?

JENNY: It's not like I did it on purpose, Jamie. If you're so upset, next time make up your own plan.

TOTLE *(to Sophie)*: We're the only ones dancing.

MISSI *(to Dover)*: You have no rhythm.

> *TOTLE, SOPHIE, MISSI, and DOVER separate and join their cabinmates.*

PLAY DOUGH: It would have worked had you just followed the plan with Jamie.

SMELLY: What are you talking about? There was no plan with Jamie or Slimey or anyone else! I liked Slimey, she liked me, and then you jumped in with your stupid camp rules!

> *SARA and RICK, who were monitoring the dance, step in.*

RICK: Alright, boys, that's enough for tonight. Back to the cabin.

SARA: Girls, you too. Let's wrap it up.

> *SMELLY storms out first, the BOYS follow with RICK. SOPHIE, MISSI, and JAMIE leave with SARA to catch up with MELMAN, SLIMEY, and JENNY.*
>
> *Once they leave, the door slams, the lights go out, and the atmosphere changes tremendously from a hopping dance to that of a large, vacant social hall or auditorium.*
>
> *TJ and CAPTAIN continue singing in a spotlight, hopelessly enamored by one another.*

CAPTAIN & TJ:
SLOW SONG
YOU CAN PLAY A SLOW SONG
'CAUSE YOU JUST CAN'T GO WRONG

CAPTAIN & TJ (CONT'D):
WHEN YOU PLAY A SLOW SONG
YOU CAN PLAY A SLOW SONG
YOU CAN PLAY A SLOW...

CAPTAIN: I think we're all alone.

TJ: It's the magic of the Slow Song.

CAPTAIN: No. No, I mean—

TJ: Hey!?! Where did everyone go?

END OF ACT I

ACT II

SCENE 1

At the end of the Entr'acte, lights up on the theater. No longer set up for a dance, instead set up with seating and a curtained stage. It's Campstock— the annual Talent Show! MISSI is on stage finishing up her song on the flute. As she plays, focus shifts to the boys' side of the audience.

RICK: Hey, we're on deck. You ready?

SMELLY: I'm not doing it.

RICK: But all your hard work... Come on, you've got those chords down!

SMELLY: I can't. I was doing it for Slimey, and now there's just no point. She hates me.

MISSI finishes. Applause.

TJ: Wow, that girl can toot her flute! Big round of applause for Missi Snyder the fluter!

WIENER *(calling out from the boys' side of the audience)*: It's flautist!

MISSI beams at WIENER's correction. She steps down from the stage with her flute and sheet music. STEINBERG emerges from backstage to remove her music stand.

TJ: Okay, well, our next act hails from San Juan Hill. Let's give it up for Robert Benjamin with some help from his counselor, Rick!

BOYS: Smelly! Smelly! Smelly!

RICK *(standing up)*: Actually, we're postponing. Sorry, TJ.

TJ: Not a problem, Rick. We'll just plow forward then with Anita Hill's very own Jenny Nolan and Jamie Nederbauer dancing the night away!

Applause. JENNY and JAMIE, dressed in matching sequined dance costumes, get up on stage. The music starts. They begin to dance— Jenny with forced enthusiasm, Jamie with lethargy and bitterness. They speak while performing.

JENNY: Jamie! You're supposed to be mirroring me.

JAMIE: Well, look where that got me.

JENNY: Omigod, get over it. You can't expect like every guy to like you!

JAMIE: I didn't! I expected one guy to like me because you led me to believe he was totally into me!

JAMIE & JENNY: Seriously? Jinx! Omigod, you are like— Stop the music! Double jinx! I am not dancing with her! Triple jinx! How was I ever best friends with you?!?

TJ: Wow, if that was part of the act, we've got some future Academy Award winners up in heeeere!

JAMIE & JENNY: It wasn't part of the act! We hate each other for real!

TJ: That's what I like to hear... Alright then, that's it for Campstock, Summer of—!

> *PLAY DOUGH stands up, pulling TOTLE, DOVER, and WIENER.*

PLAY DOUGH: Wait! The San Juan Hill Cabin has an act. Just a little something we've been working on.

SONG #9: ALMA MATER

> *The BOYS sing in grand four-part harmony.*

DOVER, PLAY DOUGH, STEINBERG, TOTLE & WIENER:
CAMP ROLLING HILLS
OUR HOME FOR E'ER YOU'LL BE
IN THE BOSOM OF THE VALLEY
SUN SHINES OVER THEE
CAMP ROLLING HILLS
FIRM OUR LOYALTY
MAY OUR HEARTS BE FILLED FOREVER
WITH THY MEMORY

PLAY DOUGH: Hit it!

> *The BOYS stand in a line. WIENER steps up from center, rips open his shirt, snaps off his workout pants and is wearing one of JENNY's dresses. The campers hoot and holler!*
>
> *Throughout the song, the rest of the BOYS striptease out of their clothes, each revealing one of JENNY's dresses. Once they are all wearing dresses, they perform a messy kickline.*
>
> *The campers continue to laugh and cheer!*

DOVER, PLAY DOUGH, STEINBERG, TOTLE & WIENER:
CAMP ROLLING HILLS

JENNY: Is that my—? Are those all my dresses?

DOVER, PLAY DOUGH, STEINBERG, TOTLE & WIENER:
OUR HOME FOR E'ER YOU'LL BE

MELMAN: You had so many. And Wiener asked nice.

DOVER, PLAY DOUGH, STEINBERG, TOTLE & WIENER:
IN THE BOSOM OF YOUR VALLEY

JENNY: Melman!

DOVER, PLAY DOUGH, STEINBERG, TOTLE & WIENER:
THERE IS MILK FOR ME

MELMAN: Hey, Steinberg! Jenny says keep the dress, it brings out your eyes!

DOVER, PLAY DOUGH, STEINBERG, TOTLE & WIENER:
CAMP ROLLING HILLS
MAKES ME HAVE TO SNEEZE

JENNY: Ew, no, I don't!

DOVER, PLAY DOUGH, STEINBERG, TOTLE & WIENER:
MAY OUR BUTTS BE FILLED FOREVER
WITH YOUR STINKY CHEESE

SCENE 2

SAN JUAN HILL CABIN

BOYS lounge around. Some sit on piles of clothing. There is very little floor space left un-littered. RICK enters, carrying mops and brooms.

RICK: Okay, boys, it's clean-up time. Captain Planet's punishment for the stunt you pulled at Campstock. Stripteasing is cool, just not when it's used to defile the alma mater. Grab a mop, take a broom, nobody sits till we clean this room.

PLAY DOUGH: We can barely see the floor.

RICK: Great observation, Play Dough. I leave you in charge to come up with a solution.

PLAY DOUGH: Oh, come on!

RICK exits to his counselor nook.

Fine. Wiener, fold clothes from the floor. Smelly, kick everything else under the beds.

SMELLY: No way.

DOVER: I can kick stuff under the beds.

WIENER: Smelly, you can fold with me if you feel more comfortable with that task.

SMELLY: No, I mean, I'm not cleaning. I didn't get in trouble.

PLAY DOUGH: We all got in trouble. One of us goes down, we all go down. That's how it works at camp.

SMELLY: Then how come Slimey's only mad at me? Is that also how it works at camp?

DOVER: Whatever, dude. This isn't about girls. Maybe you should have done Campstock with us.

TOTLE: Like, I get why you didn't play the guitar in your emotionally raw state, but what we did had nothing to do with her.

SMELLY: If I wasn't in the mood to play the guitar why would I be in the mood to sing the alma mater... in a dress... in front of the entire camp!?!

PLAY DOUGH: It wouldn't hurt you to show some spirit. You're part of this cabin too.

SMELLY: I wish I wasn't!

PLAY DOUGH *(pushes Smelly)*: Oh, yeah?

SMELLY *(pushes him back)*: Yeah!

STEINBERG: Quit fighting— you guys are friends.

TOTLE: A true friend stabs you in the front.

RICK *(emerging from his counselor nook)*: Hey, hey!

PLAY DOUGH: I pushed him, Rick, but I did not stab him.

DOVER: In the front or the back.

RICK: What is going on with you guys?

STEINBERG: Holy Dude-a-cris! I got it! Nothing is going on with us— the girls are the ones to blame. Without them none of this would have happened.

PLAY DOUGH: Yeah, it's not our fault, Rick.

TOTLE: They're driving a wedge between us.

WIENER: They're making us act crazy!

DOVER: Are you thinking what I'm thinking, Play Dough?

PLAY DOUGH: That there's double grilled cheese for lunch?

DOVER: No! The girls should pay for this.

SMELLY: Pay for what?

PLAY DOUGH: There's only one way we can bring this group back together again. Dover?

DOVER: An all-out raid on Anita Hill.

BOYS: Yeah!

RICK: No, guys, come on— you know you're not allowed in the girls' cabin.

STEINBERG: Please. Look at us, suffering.

DOVER: We need this, Rick. And we need it bad.

PLAY DOUGH: Think back to when you were a camper. Don't deprive us of what is your most treasured camp memory.

RICK: We never had this conversation and I was napping when you left the cabin.

BOYS: Yeah! Raid! Raid! Raid!

DOVER: Alright, gather round. War council time.

SMELLY: Okay... but guys, what is a raid, exactly?

SONG #10: RAID

Scenes in motion...

DOVER:
A RAID
IS A CHANCE FOR DEFENSE
AND IT'S REALLY INTENSE
IT'S THE PERFECT REVENGE
FOR THE CRIME THAT HAS TERRIBLY WRONGED US
AND TORN US APART

PLAY DOUGH:
SO IT'S FINALLY TIME WE GOT BACK AT THOSE HORRIBLE GIRLS
FOR THE GAMES THEY'VE PLAYED
SETTING US OFF LIKE A HAND GRENADE

DOVER:
NOW THEY WILL RUE THE MISTAKES THEY'VE MADE
AS UNITED WE STRIKE WITH OUR RAID...

DOVER & PLAY DOUGH:
RAID...

DOVER, PLAY DOUGH & STEINBERG:
RAID...

DOVER, PLAY DOUGH, STEINBERG, TOTLE & WIENER:
RAID!

DOVER:
MARCH ON!
COME AND JOIN THE BRIGADE
FOR THE ULTIMATE RAID
ALL THE COUNSELORS WILL THINK THAT WE'RE OFF ON AN INNOCENT
WOODS HIKE
WHILE THEY'RE ALL AT THE POOL

TOTLE:
BUT AS THEY SWIM WE WILL STEALTHILY MAKE OUR ASCENT
UP ANITA HILL

STEINBERG:
TRASH ALL THEIR STUFF TO ENFORCE OUR WILL

WIENER:
STEAL THEIR DEODORANT FOR A THRILL

DOVER:
THEN WE'LL PROUDLY MARCH HOME FROM OUR RAID...

DOVER & PLAY DOUGH:
RAID...

DOVER, PLAY DOUGH, STEINBERG & WIENER:
   RAID...
ALL BOYS:
   RAID... RAID!

"Raid" music vamps under dialogue.

DOVER: Alright men, fall in. Prepare your stations. Steinberg... intelligence.
   What do you know?

STEINBERG: On the outside, their cabin looks like ours. But in regard to the
   inside, I'd reckon it's cleaner.

WIENER: We'll see about that.

STEINBERG: Yes, we will.

RICK: Wait! Guys. I'm throwing in one rule. No touching the counselor's things.
   Got it?

DOVER: Check. Play Dough, what's the status on Weapon Number 2?

PLAY DOUGH: I think I have it in me.

STEINBERG: Good.

RICK: Okay, two rules. Keep it in the toilets.

DOVER: Yes, sir. Okay, Wiener— toilet paper. Everywhere.

WIENER: On it.

DOVER: Totle— shaving cream. Everywhere.

RICK: Not taking mine.

DOVER: Understood. We'll take the girls'.

TOTLE: Destroy the enemy with their own weapon. I like it.

DOVER: And Smelly... very important. You be the lookout.

SMELLY: The lookout? You mean, I can't—

WIENER: Well, somebody has to stand guard in case the girls come back.

SMELLY: Why can't you do it?

WIENER: Because I am in charge of toilet paper.

DOVER: Can we trust you with this responsibility, Sergeant Smelly?

PLAY DOUGH: Congrats on the promotion.

SMELLY: Fine.

DOVER: Good. Everybody ready? Let's move out.

   *The BOYS grab their supplies and march to outside Anita Hill
   Cabin. "Raid" continues.*

   (Singing)
   WE'LL BREACH
   WHEN I SEND OUT THE SIGN

DOVER (CONT'D):
  YOU'LL FALL INTO A STRAIGHT LINE

PLAY DOUGH:
  WIENER YOU'LL DO THE T.P. AND I'LL DO MY THING IN THE TOILETS

TOTLE (*while shaking shaving cream*):
  BUT NOT ANYWHERE ELSE

PLAY DOUGH: Right.

DOVER:
  STEINBERG'LL PILFER THE CUBBIES AND BEDS
  WHILE I FIREBOMB SILLY STRING
  SMELLY STAND GUARD BY THE TIRE SWING
  SOUND THE ALARM IF THERE'S ANYTHING
  THAT COULD THWART OUR ENDEAVOR TO RAID...

ALL BOYS:
  RAID... RAID... RAID... RAID!

INSTRUMENTAL

The BOYS have arrived at Anita Hill Cabin.

ANITA HILL CABIN

STEINBERG: Site clear, Lieutenant Dover.

DOVER: Ready... strike!

The BOYS execute the raid.

PLAY DOUGH: Success!

BOYS: Success!

DOVER: Looking good. Men, fall out!

The BOYS march back to San Juan Hill Cabin.

BOYS:
  OUR RAID
  WAS A FILTHY SUCCESS

DOVER:
  SUCCESS!

WIENER:
  SUCCESS!

BOYS:
  WE MADE A HUGE MESS

PLAY DOUGH:
  AND I WISH I COULD BE THERE
  TO SEE ALL THE LOOKS ON THEIR FACES

STEINBERG & TOTLE:
  THAT WOULD BE SWEET

BOYS:

> AND THE BOYS OF SAN JUAN ARE AT LONG LAST UNITED
> BUT NOW WE MUST SIT AND WAIT
> TO SEE IF THE GIRLS WILL RETALIATE
> IF THEY STRIKE BACK IT WILL SEAL THEIR FATE
> BROTHERS, WE'LL HAVE NO CHOICE BUT TO
> RAID... RAID... RAID... RAID... RAID!

SCENE 3
ANITA HILL CABIN

"Raid" music underscores the scene. The GIRLS, in swimsuits, return to their cabin to find what the BOYS have done. JAMIE walks in first followed by JENNY, then MISSI, then SLIMEY, MELMAN, and SOPHIE.

JAMIE & JENNY: AHHHHH!

MISSI: Are you girls o—? My kitty poster has been vandalized!

JAMIE *(referring to the poster)*: Aw, is that a moustache?

SOPHIE: Forget about your cat poster, what's that smell? I can't breathe.

MELMAN: Ladies, it looks like we've been raided.

SLIMEY: Holy turds, you guys. They left... holy turds... in our toilets.

JENNY, MISSI & SOPHIE: Omigod, gross!

MELMAN: Alright, that's it. We gotta get back at them!

MISSI: Raid them right this second!!! Let's go, team, let's go!

SONG #10A: RAID REPRISE

JENNY: Jamie's not wearing camouflage.

SLIMEY: Nobody's wearing camouflage.

JAMIE: I'm not coming.

JENNY: You can't just not go on the raid.

JAMIE: Actually, I can do whatever I want.

MELMAN: Not today you can't! Ladies, let's move out!

> *The GIRLS march to San Juan Hill Cabin.*

(Singing)
REVENGE
TIME TO COUNTER-ATTACK
AND DELIVER SOME PAYBACK

MELMAN (CONT'D):
> 'CAUSE IT'S TIME WE REMINDED THESE BOYS
> THAT WE'RE BETTER THAN THEY ARE

JAMIE & JENNY:
> DON'T MESS WITH THE BEST

GIRLS:
> WE'RE GONNA POUNCE WITH A VENGEANCE
> 'CAUSE HELL HATH NO FURY LIKE WOMAN SCORNED
> NOTHING CAN STOP US SO BE FOREWARNED
> THE DEATH OF YOUR CABIN WILL SOON BE MOURNED
> JUST AS SOON AS WE FINISH OUR
> RAID... RAID... RAID... RAID... RAID!

SAN JUAN HILL CABIN

Music continues. The GIRLS enter to find a cabin that looks like it's already been raided.

JENNY: Omigod, it smells like boy in here.

SOPHIE: It's like they raided themselves.

MELMAN: Try not to breathe in their toxins, ladies. Quickly, what's the agenda?

JAMIE: Omigod, we should totally steal something.

SLIMEY: Well, I know what I'm taking.

SLIMEY starts rummaging through SMELLY's stuff— knows which bed is his based on the picture of him and his parents, together.

JENNY takes an accidental step into a pile of underwear.

JENNY: Ew, ew, ew! Boy boxers!

MELMAN: That's it! Boxers! You're a genius.

JENNY: At least someone appreciates me.

MELMAN: Round up all the underwear you can find...

SLIMEY *(finding Smelly's iPod)*: Bingo!

MISSI: You're taking his iPod?

SLIMEY: We are here to avenge their attack, right?

GIRLS: Right!

"Raid" music continues. The GIRLS throw their collection of boys' underwear into a big garbage bag.

(Singing)
RAID... RAID... RAID... RAID... RAID!

SCENE 4
SAN JUAN HILL CABIN

"Raid" music underscores the scene. PLAY DOUGH takes all of his clothes on the floor— his cubbies have been dumped— and lays them on his bed.

PLAY DOUGH: Hey, guys... I know I had more underwear than this.

STEINBERG: How much do you have?

PLAY DOUGH: One... one. I have one.

DOVER: Are you sure? That's a sock.

TOTLE: Oh no! My underwear's gone too!

WIENER: Didn't you lose all yours like the first week?

TOTLE: Absence makes the heart grow fonder.

SMELLY: Where's my iPod? Did they steal my iPod, too?

PLAY DOUGH: Who would want your caveman iPod?

SMELLY: Slimey, that's who.

BOYS: Retaliation!

The BOYS march with determination toward the exit.

SCENE 5 – CONTINUOUS
ANITA HILL CABIN

The BOYS are already inside, in a huddle. "Raid" music underscores the scene.

SONG #10B: RAID FINALE

PLAY DOUGH: They steal our stuff, we steal theirs.

TOTLE:
AN EYE FOR AN EYE!

DOVER & STEINBERG:
A TOOTH FOR A TOOTH!

WIENER:
A SPLEEN FOR A SPLEEN!

SMELLY: An iPod for... something!

PLAY DOUGH: Break out on three. One, two, three...

BOYS: Sauce!

The huddle breaks— each goes to work digging through a different cubby.

PLAY DOUGH: Focus! We're running out of time. Smelly, what have you got?

SMELLY: I mean, there's her left shin guard... or I could take her stamps?

PLAY DOUGH: Dude, something she'll actually miss.

DOVER: What's that? Dangling in front of your face?

SMELLY: Well, it's her locket but—

PLAY DOUGH: It looks like revenge.

SMELLY: Nah, I'll find something else.

PLAY DOUGH: Then I'll take it. Re-gift it to my mom for Mother's Day. Or better yet, melt it down and sell it for a million bucks.

SMELLY: Forget it, I'll take it.

PLAY DOUGH: Yeah?

SMELLY: My battle to fight— my locket to steal.

WIENER: They're coming back! Let's move!

> *PLAY DOUGH high fives SMELLY. He reluctantly takes Slimey's locket, and carefully puts it around his neck for safe-keeping. WIENER takes MISSI's flute. The rest of the BOYS grab a random assortment of the girls' things and exit outside as the GIRLS walk toward their cabin. They do not see each other just yet.*

BOYS & GIRLS:
OUR RAID
WAS A THING TO BEHOLD
IT WAS RUTHLESS AND COLD
BUT IT'S JUST THE BEGINNING
'CAUSE NOW THINGS ARE GONNA GET STINKY
EVEN MORE THAN BEFORE
AND WHEN THE WAR'S FINALLY OVER
THE POETS WILL SING OF OUR NOBLE FIGHT
WINNING THE DAY AS WE PROVED OUR MIGHT
THEY WERE THE WRONG ONES AND WE WERE RIGHT
SO LET'S TOAST TO OUR GLORIOUS RAID...
RAID... RAID... RAID... RAID... RAID... RAID... RAID... RAID!!!!

> *BOYS and GIRLS finally come to a head. Their tension has reached its peak. They nearly explode as they chant!*

BOYS: San Juan Hill! San Juan Hill! San Juan Hill!

GIRLS: Anita! Anita! Anita!

TOTLE: Now you'll know what it feels like to be dirty!

STEINBERG: We've got all of your toiletries!

MELMAN: Yeah, well, we've got all your underwear! Read it and weep.

MELMAN hands PLAY DOUGH a note. The BOYS crowd around.

WIENER: It's written in blood!

DOVER: Uh, I think that's lipstick.

PLAY DOUGH: "Dear boys: We had to raid you, it was only fair. Now we have your underwear. If you want 'em back, you'll do what we say. Your boxers are hidden like real far away. Your first clue, we have a hunch, is where we eat our picnic lunch."

STEINBERG: Sounds like a treasure hunt.

WIENER: Adventure-sauce!

PLAY DOUGH: It's not any sauce, Wiener. They stole our underwear. Any idea where we start, Steinberg?

STEINBERG: Uh... yeah. It's in the riddle. Follow me.

The BOYS march in a line past the GIRLS, led by STEINBERG. WIENER attempts to play the flute.

SOPHIE: Wiener's saliva is clogging up your flute.

MISSI: He's serenading me. He's actually serenading me!

MELMAN *(as Smelly passes)*: Slimey, check out what Smelly has around his neck.

SLIMEY *(storming over to Smelly)*: You took my dad's locket!?! How could you?

PLAY DOUGH: You took his iPod! What did you expect?

RICK: Whoa, whoa, chill. Keep walking, boys. I'll catch up in a minute. *(To Smelly)* Except for you.

The BOYS head out.

MELMAN: Have fun finding your underwear, princesses!

DOVER: Oh, we will. And once we do, you're gonna wish you never started this war!

SOPHIE: You started it, cheese-brain!

SARA: Alright, girls. Inside. Slimey, hang out a sec.

The GIRLS exit to inside Anita Hill Cabin. RICK stands back with SARA— they give SLIMEY and SMELLY a chance to sort it out.

SLIMEY: You of all people...

SMELLY: I had to take something!

SLIMEY: You knew how much that locket means to me.

SMELLY: But the guys—

SLIMEY: Take some responsibility for your actions, Bobby.

SMELLY: You stole my iPod!

SLIMEY: Because I was mad at you!

SMELLY: You stormed out on me! You made me look like an idiot!

SLIMEY: You ACTED like an idiot.

SMELLY: You know what? Here— just take your locket. I was gonna give it back anyway. Only took it in the first place to keep it safe. And now you never have to talk to me again!

> *SMELLY plops down, buries his head in his hands. SLIMEY waits a second, and then looks at SARA, who gives her a reassuring nod. Sara and RICK head back to their respective cabins, give their campers some space. Slimey sits beside Smelly.*

SLIMEY: Hey. Here.

SMELLY *(taking it back from her, slowly)*: You had it on you?

SLIMEY: I snuck it to the pool. Wanted to hear some of the songs.

SMELLY: Why?

SLIMEY: 'Cause even though I'm mad at you, I still like you. And I want to know more about you. You can tell a lot about a person by what songs he listens to.

SMELLY: So, what did you learn?

SLIMEY: That you have an old-school iPod with really old-school songs...

SMELLY *(smiling)*: I know. It's a 20 gig, second generation. It's my dad's old one with all his favorite songs.

SLIMEY: That's why you cared so much? 'Cause it makes you think of your dad?

SMELLY: Yeah, except, like, there's this song on here— "Michelle" by the Beatles. Every time I hear it, it reminds me of the time we played the marshmallow game together 'cause, I dunno, it was the last song I listened to before I fell asleep that night. It doesn't make a lot of sense.

SLIMEY: No, it does.

SMELLY: 'Cause I just think of— I mean, it makes me think of you. And then there's this other one— it's called "Layla"— I was listening to it when you came over to talk to me during Newcomb.

SLIMEY: You think about all those times?

SONG #11: ALL THE SONGS ON MY IPOD MAKE ME THINK OF YOU

SMELLY:
I'M UP LATE AT NIGHT
I CAN'T CLOSE MY EYES
WISH I WAS HOME IN MY OWN BED
I PUT ON A SONG

SMELLY (CONT'D):
TO HELP ME ALONG
SUDDENLY YOU'RE IN MY HEAD
THE WORDS THAT I HEAR
THROUGH BUDS IN MY EAR
HELP ME KNOW
THAT I'LL ALWAYS PULL THROUGH
I'VE GOT 20 GIGS OF MEMORIES
AND ALL OF THEM ARE NEW
ALL THE SONGS ON MY IPOD MAKE ME THINK OF YOU
YOU GAVE ME A CHANCE
THAT NIGHT AT THE DANCE
THIS IS THE SONG THAT WAS PLAYING
WE CLICKED FROM THE START
THEN THINGS FELL APART
I DIDN'T MEAN TO DO THE THINGS I DID
SO WHEN I HEAR THIS SONG
I THINK HOW I WAS WRONG
AND I DON'T WANT TO BE WRONG AGAIN... NO
I GOT 20 GIGS OF MEMORIES
BUT SOME OF THEM ARE BLUE
ALL THE SONGS ON MY IPOD MAKE ME THINK OF YOU

I'M IN A KERFUFFLE
'CAUSE EVEN ON SHUFFLE
I CAN'T GET YOU OUT OF MY MIND
IF IT'S RAP, ROCK OR REGGAE
DON'T MATTER WHAT I PLAY
YOU'RE IN EVERY LYRIC I FIND
I'VE GOT 20 GIGS OF MEMORIES
AND ALL OF THEM ARE TRUE
ALL THE SONGS ON MY IPOD MAKE ME THINK OF YOU

INSTRUMENTAL

They slow-dance. SLIMEY kisses SMELLY on the cheek.

SLIMEY:
I PUT ON MY BACKLIGHT
SO I CAN SEE ALL NIGHT
THE SONGS THAT REMIND ME OF YOU

SLIMEY & SMELLY:
>IF IT'S SALSA
>MERENGUE
>OR PUNK ROCK
>OR BROADWAY
>IT'S YOU WHO WILL ALWAYS SHINE THROUGH.
>I'VE GOT 20 GIGS OF MEMORIES
>AND ALL OF THEM ARE YOU
>ALL THE SONGS ON MY IPOD MAKE ME THINK OF YOU.

SCENE 6

OUTSIDE

TJ and CAPTAIN converse over the PA.

TJ: Good morning, Camp Rolling Hills! Just a few brief announcements before we launch into this beautiful day.

CAPTAIN: TJ, they need you right now!

TJ: Yours truly will be joining Nurse Nannette at the infirmary to tend to the brave little boys of Bunker Hill Cabin who were singed by last night's fireworks.

CAPTAIN: On behalf of our entire staff, we apologize. They were supposed to explode in the sky.

TJ: But worry not, Nurse Nanette tells me the Bunker Boys will be back to playing games and NOT LISTENING TO THEIR COUNSELORS soon enough.

CAPTAIN: You... don't have to include this incident in your letter home if you don't want.

TJ: That's right. Take the day off from letter-writing!

CAPTAIN: That's not what I—

>*PA goes off with a squeal. PLAY DOUGH, dressed in all black with dark smudges under his eyes, carries a fish across the stage. JENNY enters, crying, dramatically ripping up a letter. She startles Play Dough, who attempts to hide the fish behind his back.*

PLAY DOUGH: Hey, Jenny, uh, what's up?

JENNY: I don't wanna talk about it!

>*She runs away crying. PLAY DOUGH stares after her, takes the fish out from behind his back. JAMIE enters, running and wheezing just a bit.*

JAMIE: Jenny, wait! Oh, hey, Play Dough.

PLAY DOUGH *(placing fish behind back)*: Oh! Hey. What's up with her?

JAMIE: Christopher dumped her. In a letter.

PLAY DOUGH: Why?

JAMIE: Probably 'cause he's intimidated by her beauty.

PLAY DOUGH: Probably.

JAMIE: Why are you carrying a fish?

PLAY DOUGH: Um, you know, lunch.

JAMIE: That's disgusting.

PLAY DOUGH: Okay!

> *PLAY DOUGH starts to leave the conversation.*
>
> *He trips on his way out, scrambles to recover, then hides behind the rock that JENNY is sitting on. JAMIE walks over to Jenny, trying to piece together the torn letter.*

JAMIE: I'm sorry about Christopher.

JENNY: No, you're not. You hate me. You're probably glad.

JAMIE: Omigod, am not. You're my best friend. Like BFF Forever Best Friend.

JENNY: So... you're not mad at me anymore?

JAMIE: Over a stupid boy who never liked me to begin with? No way.

JENNY: I'm sorry I pushed you to get a boyfriend.

JAMIE: It's okay. You only wanted me to have what you had.

JENNY: Can we never let any boy ruin our friendship again?

JAMIE: Never never!

SONG #12: CHICKS BEFORE BOYS

> *(Singing)*
> YOU'RE THE COOLEST SMARTEST
> AWESOMEST PRETTIEST GIRL I KNOW
> SO WHEN YOU GOT A BOYFRIEND
> I THOUGHT THAT I SHOULD FOLLOW
> BUT NOW IT'S CLEAR
> BOYS DISAPPEAR
> EVEN IF THE PLAN IS CLEVER
> BUT BFFS ARE SHE-F-FS
> AND FRIENDSHIPS ARE FOREVER

> *JAMIE and JENNY get up from the rock and move downstage. PLAY DOUGH slowly rises from behind the rock, watching the girls.*

JAMIE (CONT'D):
  IT'S GOTTA BE SISTERS, NOT BROTHERS
JENNY:
  FATHERS AFTER MOTHERS
JAMIE:
  UNCLES LESS THAN AUNTS
PLAY DOUGH:
  AND SKIRTS INSTEAD OF PANTS

JAMIE & JENNY: Play Dough! Get out of here!

PLAY DOUGH: Alright, alright! I'm going...

PLAY DOUGH exits with the fish.

JAMIE & JENNY:
  AND IF WE STICK TOGETHER
  THERE'S NO PROBLEM WE CAN'T FIX
  IT'S GOTTA BE CHICKS
  BEFORE BOYS

JAMIE: You hear that, Play Dough? Chicks before boys!!!

JENNY:
  YOU'RE THE SWEETEST CUTEST SILLIEST LOYALEST GIRL I KNOW
  SO WHEN I HAD A BOYFRIEND
  I WANTED YOU TO FOLLOW
  I DIDN'T THINK
  THAT BOYS COULD STINK
  UNTIL ONE DUMPED ME IN A LETTER
  BUT NOW I SEE, AND YOU'LL AGREE
  THAT GIRLS ARE SIMPLY BETTER

JAMIE & JENNY:
  IT'S GOTTA BE SISTERS, NOT BROTHERS
  FATHERS AFTER MOTHERS
  UNCLES LESS THAN AUNTS
  AND SKIRTS INSTEAD OF PANTS
  AND IF WE STICK TOGETHER
  THERE'S NO PROBLEM WE CAN'T FIX
  IT'S GOTTA BE CHICKS
  BEFORE BOYS
  AND IF YOU EVER GET ANOTHER BOYFRIEND
  AND HE TELLS YOU THAT HE LOVES YOU
  YOU CAN TELL HIM THAT YOU LOVE HIM BACK
  BUT SECRETLY YOU'LL REALLY LOVE ME MORE
  'CAUSE IT'S GOTTA BE SISTERS, NOT BROTHERS
  FATHERS AFTER MOTHERS

JAMIE & JENNY (CONT'D):
> UNCLES LESS THAN AUNTS
> AND SKIRTS INSTEAD OF PANTS
> AND IF WE STICK TOGETHER
> THERE'S NO PROBLEM WE CAN'T FIX
> IT'S GOTTA BE CHICKS
> CHICKS
> IT'S GOTTA BE CHICKS
> BEFORE BOYS

SCENE 7
THE SUPPLY CLOSET

SARA: Really, Rick? A dead fish.

RICK: You're the one who initiated a treasure hunt, Sara.

SARA: Um, since when is dirty underwear treasure?

RICK: Oh, it's treasure when you have six 12 year-olds walking around the bunk with no pants on!

SARA: You gotta come get the fish.

RICK: Not until you give back the underwear.

SARA: Not a chance!

> *They yell over each other.*
>
> *(Simultaneous with Rick)*

My girls will not sleep in their cabin tonight, I promise you that. Sophie's been so crazy, she's been keeping her epi pen in a ready to stab position, duct-taped to her thigh! Remember when I said Karma is on your side because you left my stuff alone? Well, unfortunately dead fish smell infiltrates everything. So, you're gonna need to get one of your boys back in Anita Hill to remove that stinking nemesis before I—

RICK *(simultaneous with Sara)*: My boys haven't had a clean pair in almost a week. They won't participate in any activity other than your nonsensical hunt. The clues are meaningless— it's like you wrote whatever arbitrary rhyme popped into your head. It's ridiculous!

> *SARA's rant outlasts RICK's. Rick stops his and kisses Sara.*
> *She shuts up.*

SARA: What the heck was that?

RICK: I don't know. I've seen it in movies before. Usually it works, but I guess this isn't a movie so...

> *SARA kisses him back.*

SCENE 8
ANITA HILL CABIN

PLAY DOUGH and DOVER enter, carrying the girls' toiletries, the clothes and accessories they stole, and Jenny's dresses they wore at the talent show. The GIRLS wear t-shirts and pillowcases over their faces to mask the smell. They drop the toiletries, clothes, accessories, and dresses on the floor.

PLAY DOUGH: Now, as to the matter of our underwear. I will dispose of the fish in exchange—

MELMAN: We'll exchange. Just get the fish.

DOVER: No! I did not pull an all-nighter deciphering your clues to have you hand us the answer!

PLAY DOUGH: Dude, the answer is our underfwear.

DOVER: We can do this! Don't give up, Play Dough! Never give up!

SLIMEY *(to Melman)*: I've gotta take care of something. I'll be right back.

> *SLIMEY rushes out of the cabin. Meanwhile, DOVER pushes PLAY DOUGH to get the fish. He walks through the room, to near where JAMIE and JENNY are.*
>
> *He reaches deep into Jenny's cubby, pulls out the dead fish, and parades it through the room. On the way out, he subtly passes JENNY her cell phone. She blushes.*

PLAY DOUGH *(to Jenny)*: Find a better hiding spot.

DOVER: Viva la guerra!

PLAY DOUGH: Alright, buddy, let's get you some rest.

> *JENNY's eyes are glued to PLAY DOUGH as the boys exit.*

JAMIE *(referring to Dover)*: Omigod, weird hotsauce. Jinx! Jenny, hello?

JENNY: What?

JAMIE: You're... Omigod, you were staring at Play Dough?

JENNY: Omigod, no!

JAMIE: Omigod, yes you were! You were totally staring at Play Dough. Omigod, omigod.

JENNY: He's just so fearless, you know? Like, he has no fear.

JAMIE: Sometimes fate just like happens.

JENNY: At some point, you have to stop planning it and just live your life.

JAMIE: Omigod, I learn so much from you at camp.

SCENE 9

OUTSIDE

The BOYS maniacally look for clues. DOVER is completely manic and sleep deprived.

PLAY DOUGH: Oh, let's face it, we're never gonna find 'em.

STEINBERG: I don't get it. The girls offered to give us our underwear back and you geniuses told them no?

DOVER: They have to be around here somewhere. We're so close. I can smell 'em.

WIENER: You're catching a whiff of yourself. You haven't slept or showered in like a week.

TOTLE: Dover's right. We shouldn't give up on our underwear. Our underwear would never give up on us!

STEINBERG: That is just not true.

SLIMEY enters.

SLIMEY: Hey, Bobby. Can I talk to you for a sec?

SMELLY: Oh, yeah, sure.

SMELLY walks off with SLIMEY. Meanwhile, MISSI, in disguise, sneaks up on WIENER.

MISSI: Psst. Wiener!

WIENER: Uh, yeah? Whoa. What're you wearing?

MISSI: It's time. Follow me.

WIENER sneaks off with MISSI. The BOYS, with the exception of STEINBERG, are too fixated on the hunt to notice. SLIMEY leads SMELLY to the baseball field. She stands on first base.

SLIMEY: Do you know where we are?

SMELLY: At the baseball field...?

SLIMEY: But like, more specifically?

SMELLY looks down and smiles.

SMELLY: We've reached first base, haven't we?

SLIMEY: That's right.

SMELLY leans in to kiss SLIMEY, she flirtatiously pulls back.

SMELLY *(also flirtatiously)*: First base stinks!

SLIMEY: It does, doesn't it?

Pause. Light bulb.

SMELLY: Our underwear! Is it buried below first base?

SLIMEY kisses SMELLY on the cheek, runs off.

SLIMEY: Gotta get back to the girls! Catch you later, Bobby!

SCENE 10
SAN JUAN HILL CABIN

SMELLY enters with a shovel and the garbage bag filled with their underwear.

TOTLE: Is that what I think that is?

STEINBERG: You did it! He did it! Oh, sweet, sweet undies, I thought I'd lost you forever.

WIENER: Ugh, they smell like rotten cheese.

DOVER: Where'd you find 'em? One Tree Hill Cabin?

SMELLY: Uh, yeah.

DOVER: I knew it! We eat our picnic lunch by the picnic benches which were originally outside of Notting Hill Cabin which is situated diagonally next to Harold Hill Cabin which sort of hangs over Two Tree Hill Cabin which is the rebuilt cabin after One Tree Hill Cabin got burned down by an unattended hair dryer in 1974!

SMELLY: My logic exactly.

PLAY DOUGH: Good work, Sergeant Smelly. I've gotta hand it to you— you're a cool guy.

SMELLY: I don't know about that...

PLAY DOUGH: You have a vintage iPod, a sauce girlfriend...

SMELLY: It's just, people call me a lot of things and cool isn't one of them.

PLAY DOUGH: Things are different here.

TOTLE: What Play Dough means to say is be who you are. 'Cause at camp, that's totally cool.

SONG #13: A DIFFERENT DEFINITION OF COOL

STEINBERG:
OH, THERE'S A DIFFERENT DEFINITION OF COOL AT CAMP
THERE'S A DIFFERENT DEFINITION OF COOL AT CAMP
YOU DON'T HAVE TO WEAR COLOGNE
OR GEL YOUR HAIR UP LIKE A RAMP
'CAUSE THERE'S A DIFFERENT DEFINITION OF COOL AT CAMP

WIENER:
HE'S AFFLICTED BY MYOPIA

TOTLE:
SPENDS WEEKENDS AT SYMPOSIA
PLAY DOUGH:
HE ACES EVERY TEST
DOVER:
FOR WHICH HE STUDIES FOR WEEKS.
WIENER:
AND WITH THOSE BROKEN GLASSES
TOTLE:
HE'S OUTCASTED BY THE MASSES
DOVER & PLAY DOUGH:
AND THE MASSES ALWAYS TRY TO WEDGE
HIS PANTS BETWEEN HIS CHEEKS
DOVER, PLAY DOUGH, STEINBERG, TOTLE & WIENER:
BUT THERE'S A DIFFERENT DEFINITION OF COOL AT CAMP
THERE'S A DIFFERENT DEFINITION OF COOL AT CAMP
DOVER, PLAY DOUGH, TOTLE & WIENER:
WHO CARES IF YOU WAKE UP TO FIND YOUR BED IS DAMP
'CAUSE THERE'S A DIFFERENT DEFINITION OF COOL AT CAMP

STEINBERG: Hey! That hasn't happened since I was 7!

WIENER: You mean 9!

STEINBERG: Whatever, it's not like you're so perfect, Wiener.

(Singing)
HE HAS A TENDENCY TO IRRITATE
PLAY DOUGH:
SAYS STUFF WE DON'T APPRECIATE
TOTLE:
THIS YEAR'S HIS SECOND SUMMER
DOVER:
BUT YOU'D THINK IT'S HIS FIRST
STEINBERG:
AND HIS PANTS SHOULD BE ON FIRE
WIENER:
'CAUSE I'M SUCH AN AWFUL LIAR
TOTLE:
AND WHEN IT COMES TO WOMEN
DOVER, TOTLE & PLAY DOUGH:
HE IS SIMPLY JUST THE WORST
DOVER, PLAY DOUGH, STEINBERG, TOTLE & WIENER:
BUT THERE'S A DIFFERENT DEFINITION OF COOL AT CAMP
THERE'S A DIFFERENT DEFINITION OF COOL AT CAMP

TOTLE:
DOESN'T MATTER IF YOU'RE DULLER THAN THE DULLEST LAMP
DOVER, PLAY DOUGH, STEINBERG, TOTLE & WIENER:
'CAUSE THERE'S A DIFFERENT DEFINITION OF COOL AT CAMP

SMELLY: But, how do you even know that's true?

STEINBERG: 'Cause if the standard definition of cool applied to camp, only Totle and Dover would be cool.

PLAY DOUGH: And probably me...

STEINBERG: No.

(Singing)
HE'S A MESS AND LAZY THAT'S FOR SURE
DOVER:
LEAVES CANDY WRAPPERS ON THE FLOOR
WIENER:
HE'S LOUD AND NEVER SHOWERS
STEINBERG:
AND CAN CERTAINLY EAT
TOTLE:
BUT IF YOU REALLY GET TO KNOW HIM
WIENER:
YOU WILL PRAISE THE GROUND BELOW HIM
STEINBERG & DOVER:
'CAUSE THE GROUND BELOW HIM
SOMEHOW DOESN'T CRACK BENEATH HIS FEET
DOVER, PLAY DOUGH, STEINBERG, TOTLE & WIENER:
BUT THERE'S A DIFFERENT DEFINITION OF COOL AT CAMP
THERE'S A DIFFERENT DEFINITION OF COOL AT CAMP
STEINBERG:
DOESN'T MATTER IF YOU'RE SLOW
AND PLAYING SPORTS BRINGS ON A CRAMP
DOVER, PLAY DOUGH, STEINBERG, TOTLE & WIENER:
'CAUSE THERE'S A DIFFERENT DEFINITION OF COOL AT CAMP
SMELLY:
THERE'S A DIFFERENT DEFINITION OF COOL AT CAMP
ALL:
YOU DON'T HAVE TO BE A ROCK STAR OR A FOOTBALL CHAMP
'CAUSE THERE'S A DIFFERENT DEFINITION OF COOL AT CAMP!

SCENE 11

Over the PA.

TJ: Another fantastic summer at Camp Rolling Hills is all too quickly coming to an end. We're happy to hear the boys of San Juan Hill are back in clean clothes. I was starting to feel bad gagging in their presence.

CAPTAIN: Which reminds me, don't forget to check the lost and found before you start packing.

TJ: I'm keeping everything you kids don't claim!

CAPTAIN: Uh... no. You have your own clothes.

TJ: I'm keeping them for you.

CAPTAIN: That's... sweet, TJ.

TJ: No, you're sweet, Captain. *(Taking on Captain's tone)* Now clean those cabins! You should leave camp exactly how you found it when you got here!

CAPTAIN *(taking on TJ's tone)*: But most importantly, number one... have fun! In the sun!

CAPTAIN & TJ: I love (you)—

The PA goes off with one final squeal.

SCENE 12

CAMPFIRE

SONG #14: ALL THE SONGS ON MY IPOD MAKE ME THINK OF YOU – REPRISE

The BOYS and GIRLS sit together around the campfire. JENNY and PLAY DOUGH, JAMIE and DOVER, TOTLE and SOPHIE, WIENER and MISSI, STEINBERG and MELMAN, and SLIMEY.

SMELLY stands in front of them, with RICK's guitar. He sings a reprise of "All the Songs on My iPod Make Me Think of You," and accompanies himself. During the song, JENNY leans her head on PLAY DOUGH's shoulder, he cautiously puts his arm around her.

SMELLY:
I'M IN A KERFUFFLE
'CAUSE EVEN ON SHUFFLE
I CAN'T GET YOU OUT OF MY MIND
IF IT'S RAP, ROCK OR REGGAE
DON'T MATTER WHAT I PLAY

SMELLY (CONT'D):
>YOU'RE IN EVERY LYRIC I FIND
>I'VE GOT 20 GIGS OF MEMORIES
>AND ALL OF THEM ARE TRUE
>ALL THE SONGS ON MY IPOD MAKE ME THINK OF YOU

BOYS and GIRLS applaud, cheer, whoop.

PLAY DOUGH: That was the sweetest of sauces, dude. Rick, can you teach me to play next summer?

RICK: I dunno, maybe by then Smell— Bobby can teach you.

SMELLY: You can call me Smelly. I kind of like it.

SMELLY sits down next to SLIMEY.

SLIMEY: I have chills, it was so good.

SMELLY: I meant every word. And next summer, I'm gonna sing it at Campstock.

SLIMEY: Next summer? What about baseball camp?

SMELLY: I think I'll try out for my school team instead. And I'm gonna ask my mom and dad to sign me up for guitar lessons. That way when I come back I can jam with Rick, kind of like a band.

WIENER: Speaking of bands...

MISSI hands WIENER the flute. He plays an awful rendition of the camp alma mater.

STEINBERG: That's what you were doing with Missi? She was teaching you how to play the flute?

MISSI: He's a prodigy.

WIENER: You hear that? I'm a prodigy.

TOTLE: Discovery consists of seeing what everybody has seen but thinking what nobody has thought.

SOPHIE: What about me? Can you like discover something about me?

TOTLE stares into SOPHIE's eyes, he gently moves her hair from her face.

TOTLE: You have a bugbite on your forehead.

SOPHIE sighs, consumed with love.

SLIMEY: Remember I told you— sometimes it hits you when you're home at the end of the summer and you're like—

SMELLY: "Wow, that was amazing, I'm reverse homesick, I'm campsick"?

SLIMEY: Looks like you're ahead of the game.

SMELLY: Thanks. For everything. This was the best summer of my life.

RICK: Alright, everyone, roast your last marshmallow, it's getting late.

RICK strums out a few chords on his guitar.

MELMAN: I can't believe it's over already. I'll be back in school in like T-minus 18 days. Blech.

STEINBERG: I know, blech.

MELMAN: Oh, please. You love school.

STEINBERG: Not as much as I love being here. Plus, you girls always find a way to challenge us, mentally.

MELMAN: There's just something so weird about you.

STEINBERG: Yeah, no, I'm— I'm pretty normal... average.

MELMAN: Wanna go for ice cream sometime?

STEINBERG: Yeah...!

PLAY DOUGH: You're not feeling sick or anything...? You know you just asked out Steinberg?

JENNY flirtatiously punches PLAY DOUGH in the shoulder.

MELMAN: Oh, I know.

STEINBERG: She knows.

MISSI: Ugh, back to living in two places.

WIENER: Back to sharing everything with my little brother.

PLAY DOUGH: Back to being the class clown no one laughs at.

JENNY: Being popular is so exhausting.

JAMIE: Back to being a Girl Scout.

DOVER perks up.

DOVER: You're a Girl Scout? I'm an Eagle Scout with 22 merit badges and additional recognition through Eagle Palms.

JAMIE: I don't know what that means. I just like sell cookies to myself and eat them.

DOVER: Cool. I like Thin Mints.

SMELLY: Back to, I don't even know what—

RICK: Hey, hey... enough with the frowning. You'll all be back. And if you miss this place, all you have to do is think about the fun you had, the friends you've made, and you'll warm yourself up even on the coldest, darkest winter day.

SARA: You are such a sap!

SONG #15: *IT'S ALWAYS SUMMER SOMEWHERE*

RICK:
WELL THE SUMMER IS OVER
SO IT'S TIME TO PACK UP AND GO

RICK (CONT'D):
> AND IT'S SAD TO BE LEAVING
> BUT YOU'LL ALL BE BACK BEFORE YOU KNOW
>
> ALTHOUGH THE SUN HAS SET
> IT'S ONLY MORNIN' YET
> OUT IN PHUKET
> AND DONT FORGET
> THAT IT'S ALWAYS SUMMER SOMEWHERE

SARA:
> SOON THE LEAVES'LL BE CHANGING
> AND THE GREEN WILL TURN TO RED AND GOLD

RICK & SARA:
> AND THE NIGHTS WILL BE LONGER
> AND THE TEMPERATURE WILL BE SO COLD
> BUT WHEN IT STARTS TO FREEZE
> IT'S NINETY-EIGHT DEGREES DOWN IN SYDNEY
> AND CAN'T YOU SEE
> THAT IT'S ALWAYS SUMMER SOMEWHERE
> IN VENEZUELA THEY WILL NEVER HAVE A WHITE CHRISTMAS
> ON THE EQUATOR IT IS SUMMER EVERY DAY
> EVEN THE ESKIMOS GET TO WARM THEIR TOES
> FOR A WEEK OR TWO
> AND SO DO YOU
> AS THE SNOW JUST MELTS AWAY

RICK:
> SO IT'S BACK TO YOUR HOMEWORK
> AND YOUR TEACHERS AND YOUR LONELY BEDROOM

SARA:
> AND IT'S HARD TO BELIEVE IT
> 'CAUSE YOU KNOW THE SUMMER ENDED WAY TOO SOON

RICK & SARA:
> THOUGH IT'S A CLOUDY DAY
> THE SUN IS OUT TO PLAY
> IN ZIMBABWE
> IT'S OUT TO STAY
> AND IT'S ALWAYS SUMMER SOMEWHERE

CAMPERS & STAFF:
> YEAH IT'S ALWAYS SUMMER SOMEWHERE

SONG #16: ROLLING HILLS REPRISE – FINALE

STEINBERG & SMELLY:
BACK TO BEING ROBERT

MELMAN:
STACY

PLAY DOUGH:
BRIAN

TOTLE:
JUSTIN

DOVER:
BENJAMIN

MISSI:
MELISSA

WIENER:
ERNIE

SLIMEY:
STEPHANIE

JAMIE & JENNY:
BACK TO BEING SEPARATE

SOPHIE & STEINBERG:
BACK TO BEING NO ONE

MISSI & WIENER:
AND NOBODY UNDERSTANDING ME

CAMPERS & STAFF:
NO MORE HOT WEATHER

NO MORE ALL TOGETHER

IT MIGHT SEEM FOREVER

BUT IT'S JUST AROUND THE BEND

TILL WE'RE BACK HERE WITH OUR FRIENDS

THEN WE'LL SEE THOSE ROLLING HILLS

THE SUN IS SHINING, I GOT CHILLS

WE'LL WAIT FOR TEN LONG MONTHS

SLIMEY:
TILL SCHOOL IS OUT AT LAST

SMELLY:
I'LL BE BACK NEXT YEAR

CAMPERS & STAFF:
(YEAH...! YEAH!)

FOR ANOTHER SUMMER AT CAMP

YEAH, ANOTHER SUMMER AT CAMP

CAMPERS & STAFF (CONT'D):
    IT'S ALWAYS SUMMER SOMEWHERE
    FOR ANOTHER SUMMER AT CAMP
    YEAH, ANOTHER SUMMER AT CAMP

    IT'S ALWAYS SUMMER SOMEWHERE
    FOR ANOTHER SUMMER AT CAMP
    YEAH, ANOTHER SUMMER AT CAMP
SMELLY:
    YEAH, IT'S ALWAYS SUMMER SOMEWHERE.

END OF PLAY

PROP LIST

- Large trunk
- Big backpack
- Wheel-less trunk
- Inhaler
- "Howling at the Sun" by Georgina Whitefoot (not a real book)
- "Howling at the Sun, Part 2" by Georgina Whitefoot (not a real book)
- Acoustic guitar
- Camp clothes
- A bag of marshmallows
- Licorice string
- EpiPen (or a fanny pack where it might be)
- Jacks
- Highlighter
- Locket
- Cell phones (2)
- Job Chart
- Pens
- Paper
- Envelope
- Stamp
- Postcard
- Slim Jim
- Laundry bin
- Chalk
- Original iPod
- Headphones
- Volleyball
- Bread
- Red cape

PROP LIST (CONT'D)

- Microphones (2)
- Flute
- Music Stand
- Sheet music
- Piano or keyboard
- Mops (2 or 3)
- Brooms (2 or 3)
- Shaving cream
- Silly string
- Toilet paper
- Boys' boxers
- Photograph of Bobby and his parents
- Garbage bag
- Sock
- Shin guard
- A note
- A letter
- A fish
- Toiletries
- Girls' accessories
- First base
- Shovel
- S'mores
- Roasting Sticks

STEELE SPRING
STAGE RIGHTS

ABOUT STAGE RIGHTS

Based in Los Angeles and founded in 2000, Stage Rights is one of the foremost independent theatrical publishers in the United States, providing stage performance rights for a wide range of plays and musicals to theater companies, schools, and other producing organizations across the country and internationally. As a licensing agent, Stage Rights is committed to providing each producer the tools they need for financial and artistic success. Stage Rights is dedicated to the future of live theatre, offering special programs that champion new theatrical works.

To view all of our current plays and musicals, visit:

www.stagerights.com

Made in the USA
Columbia, SC
05 March 2018